ELIZABETH BISHOP

SANDRA BARRY

Copyright © 2011, Sandra Barry
All rights reserved. No part of this book may be reproduced, stored in a retrieval system or transmitted in any form or by any means without the prior written permission from the publisher, or, in the case of photocopying or other reprographic copying, permission from Access Copyright, 1 Yonge Street, Suite 1900, Toronto, Ontario M5E 1E5.

Nimbus Publishing Limited
3731 Mackintosh St, Halifax, NS B3K 5A5
(902) 455-4286 nimbus.ca

Printed and bound in Canada

Author photo: Laurie Gunn
Design: Jenn Embree
Cover photo: Elizabeth Bishop at Balmoral Grist Mill, NS, 1976. Photo by Ernest Sutherland. Used with permission.

Library and Archives Canada Cataloguing in Publication

Barry, Sandra, 1961-
    Elizabeth Bishop : Nova Scotia's "home-made" poet / Sandra Barry.
(Stories of our past)
Includes bibliographical references and index.
ISBN 978-1-55109-823-4

1. Bishop, Elizabeth, 1911-1979. 2. Poets, American—20th century—Biography. 3. Poets, American—Nova Scotia—Biography. I. Title. II. Series: Stories of our past (Halifax, N.S.)

PS3503.I785Z54 2011   811'.54   C2010-908145-5

Nimbus Publishing acknowledges the financial support for its publishing activities from the Government of Canada through the Canada Book Fund (CBF) and the Canada Council for the Arts, and from the Province of Nova Scotia through the Department of Communities, Culture and Heritage.

ELIZABETH BISHOP

Nova Scotia's "Home-made" Poet

SANDRA BARRY

ACKNOWLEDGEMENTS

I want to thank Brenda Barry, Helen Cannon, and Janet Baker for reading an early draft of this book, locating many infelicities and, most of all, for their unwavering support. Thanks to Pat Townsend, Wendy Robichaud, and Bethany Jost at Acadia University Archives, for all their help over the years and especially with the images for this book. Thanks to Dean Rogers at Special Collections, Vassar College, for invaluable assistance and support.

Thanks to Nimbus editor Kate Kennedy for all her help. Her skill and understanding were deeply appreciated. Needless to say, all errors herein are my complete responsibility.

Finally, I must thank Phyllis Sutherland, Elizabeth Bishop's first cousin, who introduced me to the Bulmer/Hutchinson family, told me many stories, and who was a careful custodian of her family's oral tradition and material heritage. My knowledge of Bishop and her maternal family is as deep and thorough as it is because of Phyllis. She has my eternal gratitude. This book is dedicated to her.

CONTENTS

Prologue:	Defining a Poet	1
Chapter 1:	Ancestors and Emigration	7
Chapter 2:	Birth and Death	21
Chapter 3:	Great Village	33
Chapter 4:	Adolescence	47
Chapter 5:	Vassar, Europe, and Early Publications	61
Chapter 6:	The Brazil Years	73
Chapter 7:	Returning to the North	87
Chapter 8:	A Poet's Stature	99
Epilogue:	"Home-made, home-made! But aren't we all?"	111
	Bibliography	114
	Sources	116
	Index	118

Elizabeth Bishop, *circa* 1916 (age five), Great Village, Nova Scotia

PROLOGUE

"AN INFINITE NUMBER OF THINGS..."
DEFINING A POET

Elizabeth Bishop sits in her *estudio* in front of her typewriter, typing quickly, intently. Smoke from her cigarette wreaths her head. The ice in the gin and tonic she sips has long since melted. The words tumble out, *A scream, the echo of a scream, hangs over that Nova Scotian village....* For two nights, almost without stopping, the words fill page after page. When she finally stops writing, Elizabeth knows this story is good; but she is not sure what to call it—"Clothes. Food. Animals."? "In the Village"? or something else? She gets up from her desk, leaves the room, and goes down the hill to the house where Lota is busy ordering the workmen around. Sammy the toucan needs to be fed and hundreds of books need to be moved into the new wing, just finished, with its brand new custom-made stove—it can get cold in the mountains.

Several months later, Elizabeth is still undecided about the title. *The New Yorker* is interested in publishing the story. It has already taken "Gwendolyn," a memoir about Gwendolyn Patriquin, a Great Village childhood friend who died when she was nine. Writing to Ilse and Kit Barker, friends who live in England, Elizabeth asks for help. Should she simply go with "In the Village"? Then she adds, "It is funny to come to Brazil to experience total recall about Nova Scotia—geography must be more mysterious than we realize, even."

Elizabeth Bishop wrote "In the Village" early in 1952, during her first full year living in Brazil. She was forty-one years old. She did not yet know that she would spend the next fifteen

W. H. Hudson, *Green Mansions* (1916)

Elizabeth read this mysterious tale of the "bird-people" of South America while at Walnut Hill School. In December 1928 she published a review of it in the school's magazine, the *Blue Pencil*, where she wrote that she wished the book was twice as long as it was and that it made her long to leave immediately for South America where she could search for those forgotten people. Twenty-five years later, she fulfilled that longing.

years there with her partner, Lota de Macedo Soares. In fact, Elizabeth's intention was to sail around the world. She stopped in Brazil only to visit friends and because, since childhood, she had longed to see South America.

When she boarded the SS *Bowplate* in New York City in November 1951, Elizabeth knew this crazy trip was important. She described her ticket as an investment. She was running away from a difficult past and running towards an uncertain future. In the middle of the most intense identity crisis of her life, Elizabeth chose an activity essential to her, one from the earliest days of her childhood: travel.

Arriving in Brazil, she was intrigued by its wondrous and ordinary sights and sounds, and by the warmth of the people. In December, when she became seriously ill from an allergic reaction to the fruit of the cashew (she wrote to her New York doctor Anny Baumann, "I didn't know one *could* swell so much."), Lota cared for her tirelessly until she was well. To Elizabeth's surprise, exotic Brazil actually reminded her of Nova Scotia. Suddenly, after a long drought, she was writing again, writing about the very past she was fleeing. By September 1952, she had decided to stay and live with Lota. In her letters to friends

Estudio

One of the first things Lota de Macedo Soares did for Elizabeth Bishop was build her a studio (*estudio*), essentially, a room of her own in which to write. This studio still stands on the property at Samambaia, virtually as it was when Elizabeth lived there.

and family, she wrote that she felt happier than she had in years, as if she had died and gone to heaven, even if she did not deserve it.

In a 1978 letter to the critic Jerome Mazzaro, Elizabeth wrote, "Well, it takes an infinite number of things coming together, forgotten, or almost forgotten, books, last night's dream, experiences past and present—to make a poem." One could substitute person for poem. Our sense of ourselves emerges from everyday experiences, relationships with family and community, geography, history, and, as Elizabeth says here, our own dreams, memories, imaginations—and from art. Three years earlier, in another letter, she wrote her formula for composing poetry: "There is a mystery & a surprise and after that a great deal of hard work"—also a formula for living life.

Throughout her life Elizabeth Bishop defined herself in many ways: as an orphan, an exile, a poet by default. She referred to herself as 3/4ths Canadian, as American, as a New Englander, as a "herring-choker-bluenoser." She sometimes said she would rather have been a painter. In one of her most famous poems, she wrote, "You are an *I*, / you are an *Elizabeth*, / you are one of *them*."

Elizabeth always said that she liked to know exactly where she was on the map, and usually travelled with a compass. She left this compass with her Aunt Grace, likely during one of her visits to Nova Scotia in the 1970s.

In retrospect we can look at someone's life and see how events, people, and experiences shaped that person, and try to understand how someone defines her or himself. Such an activity, however, is only approximate because, if we agree with Elizabeth, how can we trace an infinite number of things? How can we know the mystery and surprise, even if the hard work is evident? In the 1960s, Elizabeth described herself to biographer Anne Stevenson as a naturally curious person. She said on a number of occasions that she liked to know about the lives of writers. She often read collections of their letters and biographies about them. She advised her students to read *all* of someone's work. Yet she also valued privacy and disliked the overly confessional poetry of the 1960s and 1970s, wishing some poets would keep some of their secrets to themselves.

Critics and biographers usually emphasize Elizabeth's intense need for privacy. Her natural and artistic reticence is well known and emerged from painful experiences in her life, such as the death of her father when she was eight months old; her mother's mental illness and hospitalization when she was five; her adult struggle with alcohol, which began in her early twenties; and her ambiguous suicide attempts later in life.

In the midst of such struggles, which gave her a pessimistic outlook, Elizabeth also believed that people "should be gay in spite of it, sometimes even giddy." She was grateful to have friends who made her laugh so hard that she would cry. One of the characteristics of Elizabeth's art is its sense of humour, which often verges on whimsy. Even as there are shadows—

"Home-made" poet

As important as her formal education, world travel, and poet friends were to her artistic development, Elizabeth's childhood in Great Village and her mother's family were her earliest and life-long influences. Her grandparents' house in the village was a home-made world. She maintained a deep respect and admiration for this time and place and these people her whole life. The idea of home-made found its way into her late poem "Crusoe in England," and is quoted on a memorial plaque to her in Great Village.

sometimes deeply dark—her sense of delight and gentle irony gave her compassion, made her humane.

This book is a brief biography of Elizabeth Bishop, one of the most important poets of the twentieth century; an introduction to a brilliant writer who, as the poet James Merrill once observed, spent her life impersonating an ordinary woman. It describes Elizabeth's ancestry, immediate family and childhood, and the principal sites of home: Great Village, Nova Scotia, and Revere, Massachusetts. It looks at her young adulthood, especially her years at Walnut Hill School and Vassar College. It follows her adult travels: to Europe, the southern United States, Mexico, back to Nova Scotia, to Brazil, and then back to New England where she lived until her death in 1979. This book also looks at the way Elizabeth Bishop is seen today and why interest in her life and art continues to grow.

Focus on the life is the *raison d'être* of biography, but it should not dominate, displace, or diminish the art. By all means, read *all* of Elizabeth Bishop's work. Biography cannot fully explain the mystery and surprise of creativity any more than it can fully explain the mystery and surprise of living life. But since, like Elizabeth, we are all curious, biography helps us understand the complex forces that affect, shape, and transform us. Though in no way complete, this book explores some of the infinite number of things that came together to create Elizabeth Bishop, a home-made poet.

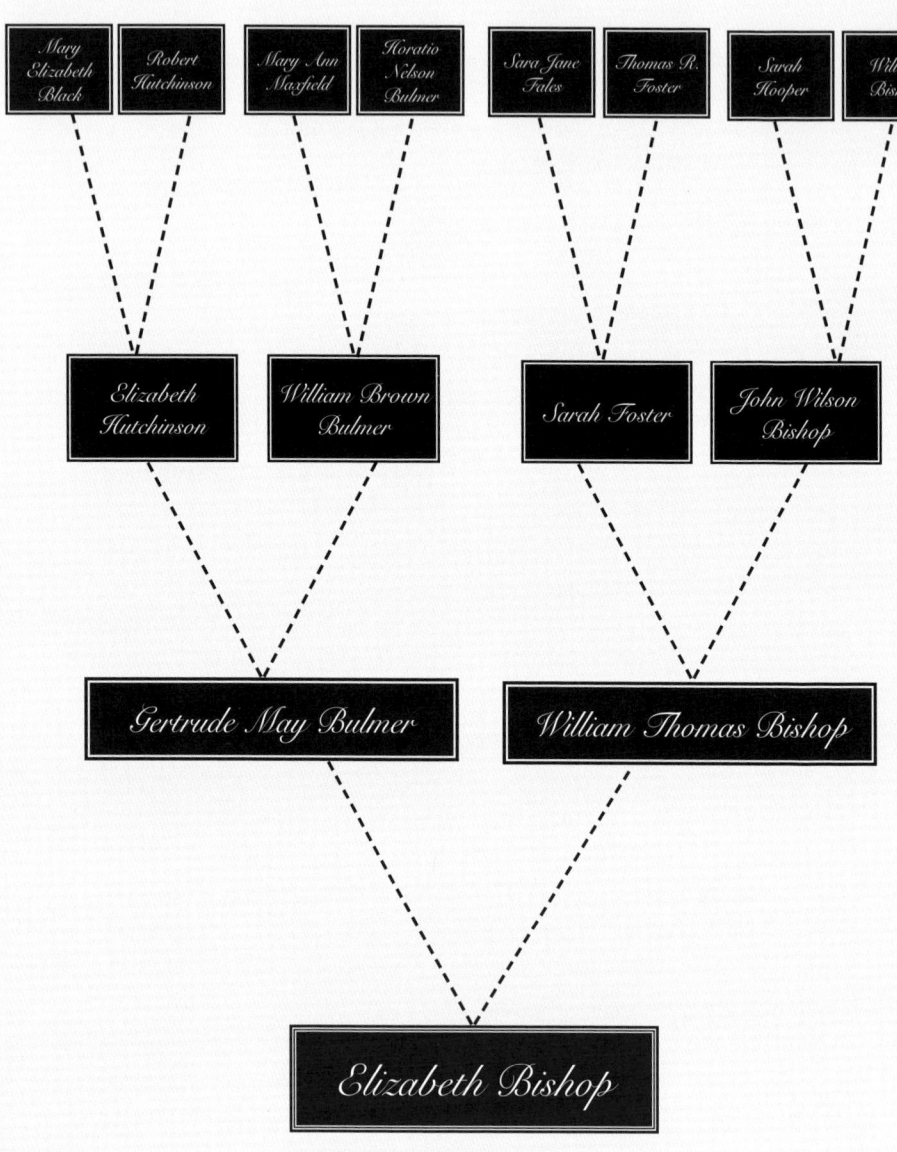

Elizabeth Bishop's ancestry

CHAPTER ONE

"THAT LINE OF MY FAMILY..."

ANCESTORS AND EMIGRATION

ELIZABETH BISHOP is generally regarded as a cosmopolitan literary figure. She travelled the world; she knew the leading writers of her day; she read the great literature of the past and translated from Greek, French, Spanish, and Portuguese. Her work has been translated into these and many other languages, including Japanese, Polish, German, Estonian, Czech, Russian, Italian, and Swedish. She was educated at Walnut Hill, a private boarding school in Natick, Massachusetts, and at Vassar College, one of the best women's schools in the United States, amid the radicalism of the 1930s and with contemporaries such as Mary McCarthy, Muriel Rukeyser, and Eleanor Clark. Her formal education was decidedly highbrow.

Her own writing covers a wide geographical area encompassing Paris, Washington, D.C., and Rio de Janeiro. Since her death in 1979, Elizabeth's stature as a major poet has solidified and critical interest in her work spans the globe. Most writing about her artistic development focuses on traditional literary influences, such as her reading of George Herbert, Gerard Manley Hopkins, and Charles Baudelaire (she once wrote that they were her favourite poets because they were like best friends); her mentorship with Marianne Moore; and her friendship with Robert Lowell. No one can deny the importance of these influences as Elizabeth acknowledged them throughout her life.

Yet, in spite of this sophisticated and far-reaching perspective, Elizabeth's artistic abilities and achievements were first and foremost a result of what late in life she called a home-

The master mariner, Elizabeth Bishop's maternal great-grandfather Robert Hutchinson

made aesthetic. Her life and art were initially and enduringly shaped by the environment of her childhood home, Great Village, Nova Scotia, Canada, and by what she called, early in her career, "a family with pets": her extended maternal family, the Bulmer-Hutchinsons.

Canadian biographer Rosemary Sullivan writes, "The mystery of our lives, of course, is that they start long before we do, determined by people whose private history we rarely know." How far back in time do we go to understand who we are now? Genealogists contend that knowing about our ancestry, near and far, is vital because character traits are transportable—and genetics has affirmed this as fact. Elizabeth had a keen interest in her ancestors and occasionally appealed to her aunts for information about family history. She told stories about her eccentric forebears to friends and interviewers right up until the end of her life.

Another question: Is an artist born or made—or some combination of the two? When Elizabeth's ancestral and immediate family is accounted for, it is clear that she emerged not from a background of "provincialism, barefeet, suet puddings, [and] unsanitary school slates," or that her artistic brilliance was the result only of that highbrow education, important as it was. Rather, she emerged from a creative lineage that provided both the genes and the upbringing needed for an artist in the house.

It is not possible here to explore fully Elizabeth Bishop's extensive ancestry, but some of the most important people in this historical collective are introduced and the way her ancestral lines converged is explained. Also described here are two major historical forces that shaped Elizabeth's ancestors' lives and, consequently, her own: the link between Nova Scotia and New England, and the phenomenon of migration.

Trying to sort out ancestry can be bewildering: as we move further back in time, there are exponentially more people to account for. Our two parents become four grandparents, who become eight great-grandparents, who become sixteen great-great-grandparents—not to mention all the great-aunts and uncles and cousins twice removed. Genealogists enjoy wading in this massive gene pool, meticulously recording names, dates, and links. For most of us, however, it is the stories about our ancestors that hold meaning.

Elizabeth was told many stories about her family history. Based as they were on oral tradition, the information was sometimes fragmentary. As the years passed, she misremembered or, as she occasionally observed, just forgot the facts. What is important, however, is that her family history mattered to her. It helped shape her identity, whether she accepted a trait, such as the wanderlust she saw in the Hutchinson line, or eschewed a trait, such as the business acumen of the Bishop line.

The four immediate family lines about which Elizabeth was most aware were the Fosters, the Bulmers, the Bishops, and the Hutchinsons. Her ancestors were predominantly English and emigrated from England to New England or the Maritime Provinces at various points, beginning in the seventeenth century. She was part of a vast human network that was constantly on the move and somehow (through chance, fate, purposeful intention) converged at the point in time when she was born. The following family sketches are done in the order of first arrival in North America.

Sarah Foster Bishop, Elizabeth Bishop's paternal grandmother (centre)

THE FOSTERS

The Foster name can be traced to the Kings of Flanders and appeared in England as far back as the ninth century. The first recorded Foster to cross the Atlantic was Reginald (or Reynold) Foster, born around 1595 in Barton, England. He arrived in New England in 1635 with his wife and children, settling in Ipswich in 1638. He married two more times and died in 1681. Elizabeth's line is traced to Thomas R. Foster, born in 1822. He married Sarah Jane Fales in the 1840s. One of their daughters was Sarah A. Foster, born in 1849. This unbroken line of Fosters was disrupted when Sarah married John W. Bishop on January 4, 1870.

Sarah Foster Bishop, Elizabeth's paternal grandmother, had great pride in her old New England stock. Some of her ancestors fought with enough distinction on the American side of the Revolutionary War that her daughter Florence applied for and was granted membership in the National Society of the Daughters of the American Revolution. Elizabeth remembered her grandmother's attempt to instill patriotism in her by making her recite all the stanzas of "The Star-Spangled Banner" over and over. Most of the words of this anthem made no sense to little Elizabeth, but the line "Between his loved home and war's dissolution" made her think of her dead father and, as she wrote years later, "conjured up strange pictures in my mind."

THE BULMERS

The Bulmer name can be traced to Anglo-Saxon settlement in England before the Norman Conquest. By the late fifteenth century, the Bulmers were a powerful family in Yorkshire; but in the 1530s the family fell from grace and lost their lands during the reign of Henry VIII. By the early eighteenth century, the Bulmers ploughed the fields they once had ruled. One of the first of this family to cross the Atlantic was John Bulmer, born in Scackleton in the late 1740s. He came to Nova Scotia with his wife, Grace, four brothers, and a sister during the Yorkshire emigration of 1772–1775. John and Grace had eight children. After Grace died, John remarried Sarah Meade (her father was a Loyalist during the American Revolutionary War). They, too, had eight children, including Horatio Nelson, born around 1803. He married Mary Ann Maxfield. They had ten children, including William Brown, Elizabeth's maternal grandfather, born in 1846 in Williamsdale, Nova Scotia.

Mary Ann Maxfield Bulmer, Elizabeth Bishop's maternal great-grandmother

As a child Elizabeth was told many stories about her grandfather's family, some of whom had remained on the original land grants in the Cobequid Mountains and some of whom had

Bulmer

Elizabeth's maternal family's surname had multiple spellings. It can be found on land grants and deeds from the colonial period as Bulmer, Bulmore, and Bullmer. By the turn of the twentieth century the spelling had settled to either Bulmer or Boomer. Elizabeth's family used both versions. Though Elizabeth preferred Bulmer, she used Boomer as the name of a character in her story "The Sea & Its Shore."

vanished into the wilderness of the American West. She never visited her grandfather's ancestral home, deep in Cumberland County, but she vividly remembered that one of her grandfather's "cousins, very rustic, used to appear once or twice a year when I was small, with gifts of bear meat and venison, in sacks in the back of the buggy."

THE BISHOPS

Little is known of the ancestry of Elizabeth's direct Bishop line. Bishops appeared in North America in the 1600s and came to Nova Scotia during the Planter immigration of the 1760s, but Elizabeth's family did not originate from these early settlers. Her line is traced to William Bishop, born in Plymouth, England, in 1809. He crossed the Atlantic with his family in 1818. They settled first in Saint John, New Brunswick, and then in White Sands, Prince Edward Island. William's trade was ship carpentry. He married Sarah Hooper in 1838. Their son John Wilson, Elizabeth's paternal grandfather, was born in Prince Edward Island in 1848. In 1857 John Wilson and some of his family emigrated to Rhode Island,

John Wilson Bishop, the "aging Poseidon," Elizabeth Bishop's paternal grandfather

where he began to work in the carpentry trade. His determined effort led him to prominence and wealth by the turn of the twentieth century. Clearly ambitious, this self-made man aligned himself with old New England stock when he married Sarah Foster.

Bishop remembered her grandfather as being like an aging Poseidon, a patriarch consumed by business. In 1956 she wrote to her Aunt Grace, "Anything *artistic*, I feel positive, *couldn't* come from there [the Bishop side], even if my father did do well in high school."

THE HUTCHINSONS

The Hutchinson name is believed to be of Viking origin, appearing first in Scotland and Northumberland. Some Hutchinsons emigrated to North America in the 1630s, but Elizabeth's direct line did not derive from them. Her Hutchinson ancestry is picked up somewhat murkily with a Charles Hutchinson of Greenwich, England, born sometime in the 1790s. Little is known of this man who was perhaps a fisherman or had ties with the Royal Navy. His son Robert, born in 1816 in Greenwich, became a seafarer and master mariner. Robert married Mary Elizabeth Black in the 1840s and they emigrated to Saint John, New Brunswick, in 1848. Their first child, Elizabeth, Elizabeth Bishop's maternal grandmother, was born there in 1850. Their first son, George Wylie, was also born in Saint John in 1852. The family then moved to Folly Village, Nova Scotia, near Great Village. Two

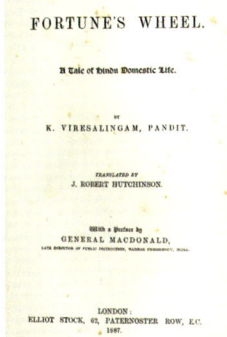

The title page of great-uncle John Robert Hutchinson's translation of *Fortune's Wheel: A Tale of Hindu Domestic Life*. Elizabeth owned several of his books, which she referred to as bad novels.

ANCESTORS AND EMIGRATION　13

more sons and a daughter were born there: John Robert in 1858, William Bernard in 1861, and Mary in 1864 (she died in infancy). It was in Great Village where Elizabeth Hutchinson and William Bulmer met and were married on September 18, 1871.

Mary Elizabeth Black Hutchinson Gourley, the Christian lady, Elizabeth Bishop's maternal great-grandmother

Of all her ancestors, Elizabeth was most fascinated by the Hutchinsons, the family most closely connected to the sea and seafaring. Her great-grandfather travelled the world's oceans in a barque. In a 1978 interview she told the writer Sheila Hale that he was "a sea captain who sailed around the Horn to Rio along exactly the same route I took when I first went there." Robert died in a shipwreck in 1866, somewhere between Sable Island and Cape Sable Island. Elizabeth believed he had written a small textbook on navigation, but it was the work of a William Hutchinson, probably an even more distant ancestor.

Elizabeth was also intrigued by her great-uncles. George Hutchinson began his painting career in the 1870s doing ship portraits and seascapes. Elizabeth's poem "Large Bad Picture" is about one of these paintings. A number of them hung in her grandparents' home in Great Village. George lived most of his life in England where, in the 1890s, he earned a name for himself illustrating the stories of writers such as Arthur Conan Doyle, Rudyard Kipling, Robert Louis Stevenson, and Israel Zangwill. George married three times, but had only two children, with his first wife.

The painter George Wylie Hutchinson, Elizabeth Bishop's great-uncle

John Robert Hutchinson sailed as a missionary to India in the 1880s with his first wife and infant son. Stories about this long voyage through the Suez Canal were told to Elizabeth during her childhood. He translated the first novel ever written in Telegu (an Indian dialect), *Fortune's Wheel*, and went on to write a number of other novels and histories (some of which Elizabeth owned). He disappeared from Nova Scotia in the late 1890s and ended up, under mysterious circumstances, in England, where he married twice more and had many children.

William Bernard Hutchinson did not have a marine connection or as varied a matrimonial record, but he had an acclaimed career as a minister, Biblical scholar, translator, and educator. He was president of Acadia University in Wolfville, Nova Scotia, from 1907–1909, the first graduate of the school to be appointed to this office. He and his wife and their two children lived most of their lives in Kansas and Iowa.

In 1964 Elizabeth observed to Anne Stevenson, "The Hutchinsons seem to have had brains, talents, and were rather eccentric." She located her own wanderlust and artistic abilities in this family. All her great-uncles were alive during her childhood and corresponding with their sister, her grandmother. Elizabeth continued to tell stories about all the Hutchinsons until the end of her life. In 1976, for example, she told the

This George Hutchinson painting became the subject of Elizabeth's poem "Poem." She owned the painting and it was known to hang in her kitchen at Lewis Wharf in Boston in the 1970s.

Dutch writer and translator J. Bernlef, "The other day I was considering that by and by I will have made all the journeys taken by my great-grandfather. Only in a more pleasant way, of course."

It is easy for us to forget how mobile people actually were before automobiles and airplanes, but the convergence of Elizabeth's four ancestral lines in 1870 and 1871 came about because of that mobility: the movements of people from England to North America, and between and within the Maritimes and New England; movements that were not only part of great emigrations and resettlements, but also motivated by individual purpose and need.

In 1933, while at Vassar, Elizabeth wrote an essay titled "Time's Andromedas," about time and the novel. In this essay

Rubato

Rubato is a musical term that refers to a temporary disregard of an established tempo—the speed at which music is played—and has the connotation of playing with flexibility and innovation. While at Vassar, Bishop studied music, so her use of the word reflects her interests and studies at that time.

she described the impact of witnessing a vast migration of birds, how she became aware not only of the whole pattern—the birds joined together by "an invisible thread"—but also of each bird separately, their "individual rubato." She realized that "the flying birds were setting up, far over my head, a sort of time-pattern, or rather patterns, all closely related, all minutely varied, and yet all together forming the *migration*."

The marriages of her grandparents in the early 1870s came about because of the forces of emigration from England to North America. From that time onward, however, the main force guiding the next convergence—the meeting of William Thomas Bishop (oldest child of John and Sarah Bishop, born in 1872) and Gertrude May Bulmer (fourth child of William and Elizabeth Bulmer, born in 1879), Elizabeth's parents—was migration.

The deep, abiding link between the Maritimes and New England (known as the "Boston States") emerged from centuries of settlement and commerce. In the eighteenth century the flow of people and trade was mainly northward, as Planters and Loyalists settled the Maritimes. By the mid-nineteenth century the flow had reversed. Industrializing New England drew Maritimers in great numbers to study and work, a phenomenon known as "out migration" (one we still know today). It was this out migration which took Gertrude Bulmer to Massachusetts at the turn of the twentieth century to study nursing. She was the first of her siblings to make this journey and was soon followed by her sisters and nieces. From then on, the Bulmers migrated regularly back and forth between Nova Scotia and Massachusetts.

    Elizabeth's bird analogy in her Vassar essay, which she applied to writing fiction, also applied to her understanding of history and geography, to her understanding of the forces (both cultural and personal) that affected and guided her ancestors and immediate family. During her life Elizabeth travelled for personal reasons, but she remained aware of the reasons why her family had travelled throughout time and space. It was the same with art. She was distinctly individual, a unique artist; but she was always aware of the creative and expressive activities and legacy of her family—and, of course, of the wider literary world. She possessed her own individual rubato, but she acknowledged her part in the time-pattern that governed her world.

The poetry gene

This poem was written by Elizabeth's great-uncle William Bernard Hutchinson in the 1890s, when he was a young man studying to be a minister. It was included in *The History of Great Village*, published in 1961 by the Women's Institute. Aunt Grace sent a copy of the book to Elizabeth when she was living in Brazil.

The Church That Faith Built

Was it folly to dyke the meadow land
    To shut out the swirling tide?
To fell the forest with calloused hands
    And build the homes that abide?

But first, in the Midst, with a faith serene
    They reared the house of prayer,
Though hardship came, and want be keen,
    God should not be wanting there!

The tide flowed in from the mighty deep—
    Flowed in with mist and rain
And bore out the sailor lads who sleep
    Far under the fathomless main.

The call of the mother across the sea—
    "Come now in hour of need,"
And they sailed away to victory—
    Those sons of the lion breed;

To victory—perchance to death,
    Some lie neath the foreign sod!
And some are lulled by the sea winds' breath;
    But some are far from God!

Church of Fathers, Church of Sons,
    Fountain of faith and power
While the tide flows and the river runs,
    Our noblest, richest dower.

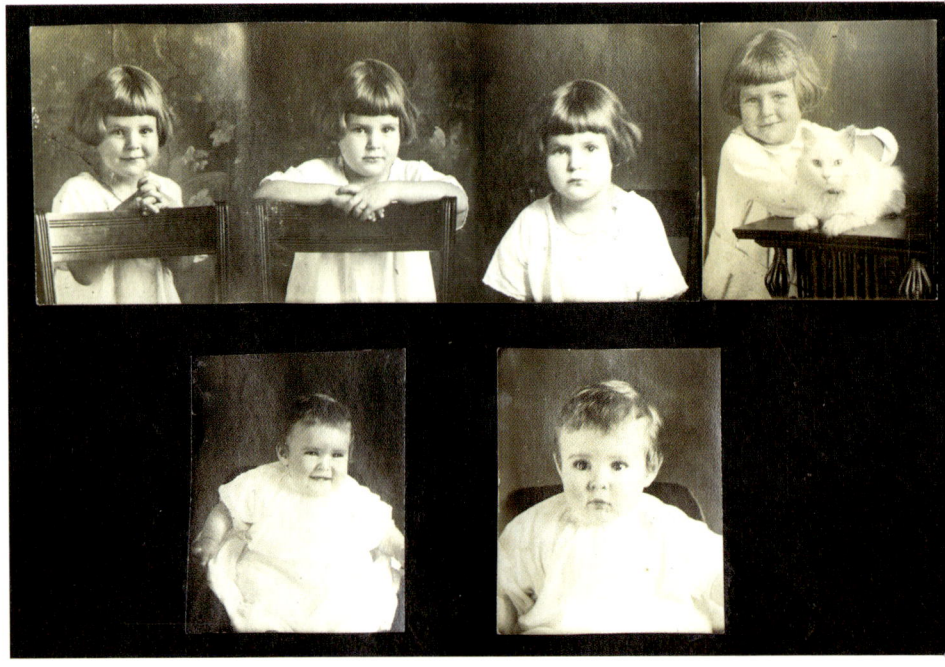

Photos of Elizabeth Bishop, as a baby and young child, by Truro photographer J. E. Sponagle

CHAPTER TWO

"THE ELEMENTS SPEAKING…"
BIRTH AND DEATH

After several years teaching school in Nova Scotia, Gertrude Bulmer decided to go to Boston sometime in 1903 for nurse's training. William Bishop was vice-president of his father's company in Worcester, a position that took him regularly to Boston. He also struggled with health problems, a result of Bright's disease, a progressive kidney ailment, which put him in hospital periodically during this time. Just when and how Elizabeth's parents met are not known, but on June 22, 1908, they were married in New York City and left immediately for Jamaica and Panama on their honeymoon. Decades later Elizabeth still had the little steamer trunks her parents used on that trip, with *Myrtle Bank Hotel* written on them.

The location of the wedding ceremony is odd. William was a well-known and respected businessman. A big society wedding in Worcester or Boston might have been expected. Gertrude's love for her family and strong connection to Great Village made Nova Scotia an equally logical choice. After all, her older sister, Maude, had married George Shepherdson in the family home in April of that year.

Elizabeth was aware at an early age that her Bishop relatives felt William had married beneath him, that he had married a poor country girl. This disapproval caused serious problems after his death. It appears that William and Gertrude eloped or, at the very least, chose an independent path away from family issues. Even so, they returned to Worcester after their honeymoon and took up residence at 875 Main Street.

Two and a half years later Elizabeth was born, on February 8, 1911. Gertrude was thirty-two years old, William thirty-nine. One of the most remarkable documents Elizabeth had in her possession for her entire life came from this time. Four days after her birth, which was a forceps delivery and caused complications for Gertrude, William wrote to his mother-in-law. This letter, quoted in full below, is the only direct glimpse into the home in which Elizabeth was born. In light of subsequent tragic events, the joy it expresses is poignant. Regardless of the traumas and troubles she faced and struggled with during her life, Elizabeth knew that at the moment she entered the world she was surrounded by love, and she knew it through her father's voice:

Elizabeth Bishop's father, William Bishop (seated), with his siblings, *circa* 1900

> Dear Ma Boomer—
> Enclosed is a bunch of hair Gertrude wanted sent you, cut from the head of the most beautiful baby born in America. She is a Yankee, pure Yankee. Has blue eyes and black hair. This morning she said "Daddy" and tomorrow will set [*sic*] up in her chair at table. Took her picture this morning and if it turns out well will send you one.
>
> Gertrude is fine, and can probably write you herself in a day or two. Has more milk than she knows what to do with, so we shall make butter probably. We started to bare [*sic*] twins and when we changed our minds forgot to cut off half the milk supply.
>
> George and Maud are so sore they won't speak to us any more. But of course they could not expect to keep up with we Yankees.
>
> Give my regards to grandpa Boomer and Aunt Mary and Grace and I trust you are getting along as nicely and happily as we are just now.
> Yours very truly, Wm Bishop

Elizabeth Bishop's mother, Gertrude Bulmer, *circa* 1900, Great Village, Nova Scotia

The happiness did not last. On October 13, 1911, William died. His death triggered a chain of events which had a profound effect on Elizabeth. The most complex and misunderstood result of William's death was its impact on Gertrude. Most books about Elizabeth Bishop account for the years following William's death and the relationship between Elizabeth and her mother in a few brief sentences: In 1916 her mother became permanently insane. She was hospitalized until her death in 1934. Elizabeth never saw her again.

Ironically, the source of this synopsis was Elizabeth herself. In 1964 she told Anne Stevenson, who was writing the first book about her:

> I think you might just as well say in the chronology: "1916. Mother became permanently insane, after several breakdowns. She lived until 1934." I've never concealed this, although I don't like to make too much of it. But of course it is an important fact, to me. I didn't see her again.

BIRTH AND DEATH   23

William Bishop with his daughter, Elizabeth, spring 1911

The years immediately following William's death were much more complex than this brief reckoning, set by Elizabeth at a moment in time because of the painful and private nature of the experiences. From what evidence remains, it is known that Gertrude tried for several years to live normally, even though she struggled with grief. Elizabeth had remarkably vivid memories of these earliest years of her life, of being with her mother in Great Village and Boston, and travelling around New England.

Then, early in 1914, Gertrude suffered a breakdown. She was hospitalized at a private sanatorium in Massachusetts for several months. In June 1914, Gertrude and Elizabeth were together again at the Bishops' summer home in Marblehead, Massachusetts, when the Great Salem Fire occurred. Marblehead is across Salem Harbor and all night they watched the city burn. Elizabeth remembered this night her whole life and tried to write a poem about it, which she never finished:

Nova Scotia Hospital (Mount Hope) in Dartmouth, Nova Scotia, was established in the mid-nineteenth century with the help of New England reformer and philanthropist Dorothea Dix. It was the only major psychiatric institution in the province during Gertrude Bishop's time there. It also housed a training school for nurses. Elizabeth told one of her friends in the 1970s that the only biography she ever wanted to write was about Dix, because she had helped the mentally ill.

> When I was three, I watched the Salem fire.
> It burned all night (or then I thought it did)
> and I stood in my crib & watched it burn.
> The sky was bright red; everything was red:
> out on the lawn, my mother's white dress looked
> rose-red…
> ….
> I was terribly thirsty but mama didn't hear
> me calling to her.

The next day, as Elizabeth and her mother walked the debris-strewn beach, she remembered:

> I picked up a woman's long black cotton
> stocking. Curiosity. My mother said sharply
> *Put that down!* I remember clearly, clearly –
> But since that night, that day, that reprimand
> I have suffered from abnormal thirst…

BIRTH AND DEATH   25

Gertrude Bishop with her daughter, Elizabeth, spring 1911

At the time of her trouble, Gertrude signed over the administration of her and Elizabeth's estates to her father-in-law, John Bishop. Problems then arose between Gertrude and her in-laws concerning Elizabeth. John Bishop had also become Elizabeth's legal guardian in 1914 and even though Gertrude recovered from her illness, he made claims for custody of his granddaughter. Upset by this pressure, Gertrude brought Elizabeth back to Nova Scotia in April 1915, apparently to live there permanently.

The four-year-old Elizabeth Bishop was brought fully into her maternal family fold where she remained for the next two and a half years. Gertrude, however, became increasingly restless and agitated. The nature of her illness is also complex. Elizabeth told Stevenson in 1964, "It has always been said that what set off my mother's insanity was the shock of my father's death at such an early age, when they'd only been married three years."

As powerful as her grief was, the tragic fact is that Gertrude also suffered from an underlying medical condition, hyperthyroidism, which was not well understood in the 1910s. Left untreated, this condition has a devastating effect on the body and the mind. In Edwardian Canada, women were expected to behave with decorum. As Gertrude became increasingly emotional and erratic, all that those around her could do was label her insane.

It must also be remembered that in 1916 the world was engulfed in the worst war it had ever seen. Like thousands of others in Canada, Gertrude was deeply affected by this spectacle and tragedy. Young men from Great Village, all of whom Gertrude knew, went to Europe. Many never returned. Gertrude was also agitated by the suffragist movement, the campaign to give women the vote. Suffragists in England and the United States were treated with suspicion and contempt. Some were imprisoned, and to protest their imprisonment, some went on hunger strikes and were force-fed.

Gertrude and Elizabeth Bishop, *circa* fall 1911

These wider social and political issues, Gertrude's grief, the custody trouble, the hyperthyroidism, and the incomprehension of those around her converged in March 1916 and caused a violent outburst, which, for the five-year-old Elizabeth, became embodied in her mother's scream. Gertrude realized she needed help and in June of that year she voluntarily admitted herself to the Nova Scotia Hospital (known as Mount Hope) in Dartmouth, Nova Scotia. She never left.

William and Elizabeth Bulmer ("Pa" and "Gammie") with Elizabeth Bishop

Almost from birth, Elizabeth's experience of her mother was that she moved around, sometimes with Elizabeth, sometimes without her. When Gertrude went off on her own, Elizabeth invariably stayed with her maternal aunts or grandparents. Always, Gertrude returned. In the story "In the Village," Elizabeth described this phenomenon: "First, she had come home, with her child. Then she had gone away again, alone, and left the child. Then she had come home. Then she had gone away again, with her sister; now she was home again." Being in the village meant that Elizabeth was connected to her mother, even when Gertrude was absent.

For Elizabeth, her mother was a force of nature: tidal, elemental. She was beautiful and frightening, natural and mysterious. As "In the Village" reveals, Elizabeth connected her mother to all the sights, sounds, tastes, smells, and textures of the village. As haunting as her mother's scream was (and it sounded in Elizabeth's imagination forever), the other sounds in the village, especially the clear, beautiful *clang* of the village blacksmith's anvil, kept the scream (and the pain) from becoming too overwhelming.

Halifax Explosion

The Halifax Explosion occurred just after 9:00 AM on December 6, 1917, when the French munitions ship *Mont Blanc* struck the Belgian relief ship *Imo* at the north end of Halifax Harbour. The *Mont Blanc* caught fire and after burning for a short time, blew up, devastating the north end of the city. The explosion is regarded as the worst non-nuclear man-made explosion in history. Nearly two thousand people were killed instantly and nearly ten thousand wounded. The north end of Mount Hope, the women's wards, was badly damaged.

After Gertrude entered Mount Hope, Elizabeth's maternal grandparents, aunts, uncle, and cousins tried to keep life as normal as possible for the five-year-old. It must be remembered that everyone at that time believed Gertrude would return. The Bulmers hoped for her recovery for years. Even after the disaster of the Halifax Explosion on December 6, 1917, which devastated the city, caused extensive damage to Mount Hope, and further destabilized Gertrude, the Bulmers continued to believe she would come home.

William and Elizabeth Bulmer, "Pa" and "Gammie" to Elizabeth, were anchors for the sensitive and precocious child. Pa was a retired tanner, currier, and shoemaker who rode around the village on his horse-drawn wagon, even as automobiles were becoming the rage. Gammie was a renowned gardener. She was active in many organizations such as the Ladies' Aid Society, the Sons of Temperance, and the Women's Institute. They were devout Baptists but not evangelical. They were gentle, practical, and kind-hearted. Their home and barn were filled with animals: cats, canaries, cows, chickens, horses, and a dachshund named Betsy, given to Gertrude the year Elizabeth was born. Gammie was the first person to teach Elizabeth to read and write. Though not her parents, Gammie and Pa gave Elizabeth love, understanding, and stability during this formative and uncertain time.

Elizabeth Bishop, *circa* 1914

Their devotion endeared them to Elizabeth for the rest of her life. They were beloved.

Family circumstances were, however, unresolved. In September 1917, John and Sarah Bishop arrived in Great Village to lay their own claim to their granddaughter. They stayed for a month at Elmonte House, an elegant hotel across the river from the Bulmer home. In early October they packed up Elizabeth's things and took her by train to Worcester. This removal from Nova Scotia was even more traumatic for Elizabeth than her father's death or her mother's hospitalization.

When Gertrude was hospitalized, Elizabeth naturally believed her mother would come back—everyone believed it. As long as she stayed home, Elizabeth would see her mother again. When the Bishops removed her from Nova Scotia, suddenly the child realized that it was she herself who was not home, so that when her mother returned Elizabeth would be gone. She would never see her mother again. The shock of this realization sealed loss and grief into a permanent condition.

This removal was the most disorienting experience of Elizabeth's childhood. Good intentioned as it was (the Bishops believed that Elizabeth would have more educational opportunities in Massachusetts), the adults in her life made decisions that

Gertrude and Elizabeth Bishop, Great Village, winter 1916

permanently affected her sense of herself, her identity, and her relationship with her mother, the most important person in her life. Decades later, in her story "The Country Mouse," she wrote:

> I felt as if I were being kidnapped, even if I wasn't….I had been brought back unconsulted and against my wishes to the house my father had been born in….It was a day that seemed to include months in it, or even years, a whole unknown past I was expected to feel I should have known about, and a strange, unpredictable future.

This removal also took her away from the only place she knew as home: Great Village.

BIRTH AND DEATH

Bulmer family home, Great Village, Nova Scotia, *circa* 1883. Left to right: Arthur Bulmer (on horse), William Bulmer, Maude Bulmer, Elizabeth Bulmer, Gertrude Bulmer

CHAPTER THREE

"THAT NOVA SCOTIAN VILLAGE..."
GREAT VILLAGE

Some of the most important people in Elizabeth Bishop's life have been introduced, but what about Great Village, the place where she spent her early years? What was Great Village like in the 1910s? As with Elizabeth's ancestry, it helps to know something about the geography and history of the village to understand her experiences there and how it influenced her life and art.

Great Village is located near the extreme eastern end of the Bay of Fundy, most famous for its powerful tides, the highest in the world. The village is a few kilometres from Cobequid Bay, an inner reach of Minas Basin. It sits beside the Great Village River, a tidal river until it was dyked in the twentieth century. The sources of the river are found in the Cobequid Mountains, which rise to the east and north and shelter the small communities running along their base.

Paleo-Indians and later the Mi'kmaq and Maliseet were the first peoples to inhabit this area. Nomadic, they came and went during their hunting and fishing cycles. The first European settlers were Acadians, who came out of Annapolis Royal in the seventeenth century. They were the first to dyke the marshes in order to farm the rich, alluvial earth. Their expulsion in 1755 made

The Bulmer family home, Great Village, 1910s

Nova Scotia and childhood were the subjects of or inspirations for many of Elizabeth Bishop's best known and most loved poems and stories. Even when a work was not directly about her past, images, ideas, and other details can often be traced back to Great Village and her maternal family.

Some of Elizabeth's Nova Scotia poems include:

"Manners"
"Sestina"
"First Death in Nova Scotia"
"Filling Station"
"Sandpiper"
"At the Fishhouses"
"Cape Breton"
"The Moose"
"Large Bad Picture"
"Poem"
"The Prodigal"
"A Summer's Dream"
"Over 2,000 Illustrations and a Complete Concordance"
"For C.W.B."
"Three Sonnets for the Eyes"
"The Reprimand"

Some of her Nova Scotia stories include:

"In the Village"
"Gwendolyn"
"Memories of Uncle Neddy"
"Primer Class"
"The Baptism"

way for successive waves of English-speaking settlers, direct from the British Isles and via the eastern seaboard of the United States, during the second half of the eighteenth century. They harvested the vast forests of the mountains and established centres of commerce. By the mid-nineteenth century, shipbuilding was underway and the great "Age of Sail" was ushered in.

Like many other communities along the Fundy shore, Great Village had a vibrant shipbuilding industry. Dozens of schooners, brigs, and barques were built during the second half of the nineteenth century. The village was also designated the Port of Londonderry, the customs centre of the area. Importing and exporting kept lumbermen, miners, fishermen, tradesmen, and merchants busy year round. The prosperity brought by all this activity was reflected in the large, elegant homes and public buildings constructed at this time.

With Canadian confederation in 1867 came the transcontinental railroad. Sailing ships and locomotives co-existed for a while, but by the end of the nineteenth century the age of the great sailing ships was over. The political and economic dominance of central Canada took industry and people away from the region. Ironically, World War I (1914–1918) brought renewed economic activity for the Maritimes, but it also claimed a generation of young men. Dozens of young men from Great Village enlisted, many were wounded, and twenty-one of them were sacrificed in the trenches in France. Yet, in spite of powerful national and global pressures, Great Village remained a thriving community in the first decades of the 1900s, solid in its traditions but also looking to the future.

Presbyterian church, Great Village, *circa* 1890s

The village Elizabeth came to in April 1915 had a population of about one thousand, which clustered around two churches: Presbyterian and Baptist. The Presbyterian church was established in the late 1700s. By 1848 the congregation was substantial enough that it built an impressive house of worship, big enough to seat twelve hundred people. This edifice dominated the skyline for decades, but in 1882 it was destroyed by fire. The determined parishioners dedicated a new, slightly smaller but still impressive church in 1884.

Great Village Baptist Church

The ceiling in the sanctuary, shaped like the inverted hull of a ship, honoured the shipbuilding industry that sustained the community. Its 112-foot steeple loomed over Elizabeth's world (the Bulmer home was right next door) and she observed decades later, "I was as familiar with it as I was with my grandmother." She remembered playing hide-and-seek among its non-flying buttresses and swinging on the chain fence that surrounded its

The Christophian Literary Society

The Christophian Literary Society was formed in the early 1900s in Great Village. It was most active in the winter months when people gathered in their parlours to discuss poets such as Shakespeare, Dante, Milton, Keats, Browning, and Tennyson. The society also held concerts celebrating the beloved Scottish poet Robert Burns. The leading member of the society was Reverend Alexander Louis Fraser, the minister of St. James Presbyterian Church, who was himself a poet and published many books. Elizabeth would have known Reverend Fraser, who continued to visit the village throughout the 1920s. Elizabeth's mother and her aunts were members of the society.

yard. The minister during Elizabeth's childhood was a Scotsman named William Gillespie, who rode around the village on a bicycle, wearing a black straw hat.

The Baptist church was officially organized in the mid-nineteenth century and though its meeting house was not as grand as the Presbyterian church, its activities were more central in Elizabeth's life, being the faith of her grandparents. She had vivid memories of attending services with her beloved grandfather and listening to Reverend F. G. Francis's sermons and the excellent choir. She remembered Reverend Francis as a kind and forbearing pastor:

A page of ads from the *Great Village High School Annual*, 1914, including one for the tinsmith business owned by Elizabeth's uncle Arthur Boomer

> One summer Sunday afternoon, all good Baptists in church, the doors open, Dr. Francis, the minister, was on his knees praying, when a patter-patter was heard and Betsy [Elizabeth's dachshund] trotted down the aisle past our pew. She was fond of Dr. Francis and went right up on the platform and jumped to lick his face. He opened his eyes and said, "Why Hello Betsy" and went right on praying.

Though as an adult Elizabeth regarded herself as a nonbeliever (or "Unbeliever," as one of her poems says), she acquired from the religious experiences of her childhood a keen interest in church architecture and an abiding love of church music. Of the latter, she often said that she was full of hymns.

In addition to religion, which spawned Sunday schools and missionary societies, Great Village also had many moral and civic organizations such as the Iron Age Division of the Sons of Temperance, the Women's Christian Temperance

Elmonte House, Great Village, 1910s

Union, the Women's Institute; fraternal associations such as the Masons, Oddfellows, and Foresters; youth groups such as the YMCA, Boy Scouts, and Band of Hope; and sports clubs connected to baseball, tennis, and sulky horse racing. The arts were also cultivated, with a chamber orchestra, theatre troupe, the Christophian Literary Society, and frequent concerts and musicales. Gatherings regularly occurred for all sorts of public and private reasons: for lectures by travelling speakers, for elections, for birthdays, weddings, and funerals, for quilting and rug-hooking bees, for services and ceremonies connected to holidays such as Christmas, Halloween, Empire Day, Dominion Day, and the king's birthday.

The most important but intangible impact of all this activity was the fostering of communal identity. The Bulmers were directly involved in most of these associations. They participated in and hosted meetings, performed in concerts, and canvassed for good causes. Elizabeth witnessed her grandparents, aunts, uncle, and cousins engaged in a wide range of socializing and through them she saw this close-knit community celebrate success, help in crisis, and grapple with the terrible reality of war.

So busy were the people of Great Village socializing and entertaining, one wonders when they found time to work, but

Great Village School and students, *circa* 1905

work hard they did: farming, lumbering, mining, fishing, and providing innumerable services for residents and visitors. In the 1910s and 1920s Great Village had a bank, three general stores, a drug store, an elegant hotel called the Elmonte, a post office, an award-winning creamery, a blacksmith, a tinsmith, a jeweller, a milliner, a dressmaker, a tailor, a doctor, a dentist, a telephone operator, a shipyard and customs office, and an electric light generating plant.

Elizabeth was fascinated with village life:

> For some reason or other I always felt that the parlor belonged to me. Although close upon the village street, so that your face, as you looked through the square window panes, was on a level with and only a few feet away from the face of a passerby, it seemed much more secluded than any other place in the house…and in the parlor was the one place where I could think about the village people and my own family as from a distance….I used to go in there and sit in a rocking chair just behind the window curtains and look out at the lace-covered view they gave me, like any curious old lady.

Elizabeth's aunt Mary Bulmer Ross, several years before she made Elizabeth late for school

She saw all manner of activity through that lace-covered view.

Being so young in the 1910s, Elizabeth's direct involvement in communal activity was centred on church and school. She received her first formal education when she attended grade primary in the Great Village School in the fall and winter of 1916–1917. Her vivid memories of this formative experience were recounted decades later in one of her most charming memoirs, "Primer Class."

The Great Village schoolhouse, built in 1904, was a shining example of the push for consolidation taking place in Nova Scotia as the tiny one-room schools disappeared. Elizabeth remembered it as an imposing structure of white clapboard, with high windows and a dark roof, on which sat an elegant cupola. She also remembered the two outhouses that sat behind it. There was an outhouse in her own backyard.

She vividly remembered her teacher, Miss Georgie Morash, who was a close friend of her Aunt Grace. She remembered her classmate Muir MacLachlan, whose first name she initially misheard as "Manure." She remembered the intriguing pull-down maps, the slates and rags, the beans sprouting in jars on the window sills, the reader she had already mastered, the urgent

Billy Francis from Great Village, in his 193rd Highland Brigade dress uniform, *circa* 1915

ringing of the school bell, and the morning Aunt Mary made her late: "I ran into the classroom and threw myself, howling, against Miss Morash's upright form….I was never late again."

One of the most important aspects of Great Village during Elizabeth's childhood was World War I. Though the battles and carnage were far away in Europe, the war had a huge impact on the home front. Most directly, it took young men away, many of them never to return. Elizabeth witnessed the early mobilizations in 1915–1916, with the parades of young men in their Highland Brigade uniforms of kilts, tam-o'-shanters, sporrans, and swagger sticks, marking the great hope that the British Empire would prevail quickly. She witnessed the first memorial services and honour rolls as one by one the young men succumbed to the brutality of trench warfare. The Bulmers lost no sons in the war, but they knew every young Great Village man who crossed the Atlantic.

Patriotic politics and rhetoric in Canada imposed a strict taboo on public grief. But, as Elizabeth remembered, communities mourned the missing and the dead anyway:

> It was during the first World War—the village boys (a kilted regiment) would come to say goodbye and their clothes were wonderful, of course. Most of them were never seen again—almost every boy in that tiny place, from 18–22, was killed in one of the big battles—Canadians first, of course—and the whole village was in mourning.

In many ways, World War I marked a major shift in global politics, economics, culture, and individual awareness. Some historians argue that the war marked a clear break with the past because innocence was lost and nothing could ever be the same. It marked an unprecedented turn towards technology, and in many ways was a force of modernity, a point when long-held traditions were shattered and abandoned. Other historians,

Temperance

Temperance was a religious and social movement supported by many people in Nova Scotia in the nineteenth and early twentieth centuries. It concerned either the temperate (or moderate) use of alcohol or total abstinence from drinking. Many societies were formed to advocate for this cause. The Sons of Temperance was an international organization with branches across Canada. Formed in the early 1850s, the Iron Age Division of the Sons of Temperance was in existence in Great Village for more than fifty years. The Women's Christian Temperance Union was also long-lived there. Elizabeth's maternal family were actively involved in both societies.

however, believe the change was not so decisive. They argue that even as new attitudes and approaches took hold, traditions were reassessed and those that still had value were reaffirmed.

Perhaps one of the most important dilemmas that Elizabeth absorbed from this time, which she took into her future, was this debate between the value of the past and the future: tradition and modernity. In fact, a vivid manifestation of each side could be witnessed in her own family: William Bulmer remained faithful to his old-fashioned horse-drawn wagon until his death in 1930.

Elizabeth's uncle Arthur Bridges Bulmer, *circa* 1884, who became an advocate for modernity in Great Village

Arthur Bulmer, Elizabeth's tinsmith maternal uncle, was one of the first people in Great Village to buy an automobile, a Model-T Ford, the harbinger of modern times.

Elizabeth was fascinated by both sides of the debate. She had deep respect for her grandparents and their close-to-the-earth, home-made way of life; but she regularly used modern transportation and communication technologies, she acknowledged the necessity of living in big cities, and she participated in commercial, even corporate, activity. She saw things to accept and reject in both tradition and modernity. She lamented the loss of traditional ways of life, not only in early twentieth-century Nova Scotia, but also in mid-twentieth-century Brazil. She felt regret and resignation towards the rapid pace of change. She

Tradition and modernity in Great Village: a horse-drawn wagon, and Beryl Smith at the wheel of one of the first automobiles in the village, turn of the twentieth century.

chose primarily to write about the past, but she also explored the angst-filled conditions of the present and the uncertainty and hope of the future.

Though she spent only a short continuous time in Great Village (from April 1915 to October 1917), Elizabeth told Stevenson in 1964, "This whole period in my life was brief—but important, I know." Part of the proof of this importance is found in the

Great Village School

Great Village School was built in 1904 and was seen as a model for consolidation. During Elizabeth's year there, 1916–1917, classes went from primary to grade eleven. One of the biggest exports from Great Village was schoolteachers. About 115 young people from the village became teachers, including Elizabeth's mother and her Aunt Grace. Though brief, Elizabeth's time there made a deep impression on her and her memories were still vivid when she wrote her memoir "Primer Class" over fifty years later. The building is still used as a school today and has been designated a Provincial Heritage Property.

dozen or so major poems and half a dozen stories she wrote that are directly based on childhood memories or set in Great Village and Nova Scotia. The numbers are all the more significant because she published only about one hundred poems (including those she wrote in her youth) and twenty stories and memoirs during her life, though she left many unfinished works, some of which are also based on the memories, people, and places of her Nova Scotia childhood.

Elizabeth Bishop's maternal grandmother Elizabeth Bulmer, contemplating modernity, 1910s

In 1963 Elizabeth described herself to Stevenson as a "late-late Post World War I generation-member, rather than a member of the Post World War II generation." The vividness of her experiences in the 1910s in Great Village had a lot to do with this view. Though she never returned to live in Nova Scotia as an adult (she did continue to visit right up until her death in 1979), she acknowledged to herself and Stevenson the importance of this time in her personal and artistic development.

Elizabeth Bishop, *circa* 1924–1925

CHAPTER FOUR
"YOU ARE AN I..."
ADOLESCENCE

In October 1917, when Elizabeth Bishop was taken to Worcester to live with her paternal grandparents, the familiarity of Great Village and the security of her mother's family was suddenly disrupted. Unaware of the legal issues that motivated the adults and prompted this action—and their genuine desire to do what was best for her—Elizabeth experienced this removal as traumatic. Decades later, in her memoir "The Country Mouse," she recounted her vivid memories of living in the large, rambling Bishop house, which felt alien and foreboding to her: gloomy, unsettled, ominous, and lowering were some of the words she used to describe it.

John Bishop was a formidable businessman who seemed distant if not unkind. Sarah Bishop was a petite but passionate patriot who took it as her principal duty to educate the six-year-old about allegiance to her native land. Also in the household was Aunt Florence, unmarried and proper, with whom Elizabeth had the longest (and always fraught) relationship of any of her father's family. Uncle Jack (John Bishop Jr.) and

The Bishop family home in Worcester, Massachusetts

his wife, Ruby, were also around. Jack became the administrator of Elizabeth's estate after his father died. They were the least sympathetic of all her paternal relatives, believing that Elizabeth had been spoiled by her mother's family. Perhaps the most difficult aspect of Elizabeth's experience with her paternal family was their silence about her mother. Talk of Gertrude was taboo.

This plaque now marks the site of Elizabeth's grandparents' house in Worcester, Massachusetts

The Bishops had several servants: a cook and maid named Agnes, a chauffeur named Ronald, and a gardener named Ed. Elizabeth felt most comfortable with them, their warmth and friendliness a contrast to the cold atmosphere in the rest of the house. She became attached to the family's dog, a Boston bull terrier named Beppo. With a touch of irony, she recalled that she and Beppo lived on the same terms in the house.

She was sent to school immediately and made a few friends her own age, particularly a little girl named Emma, to whom she lied saying that her mother was dead. But, as 1918 arrived, Elizabeth was already becoming ill. In February she experienced one of the strangest events of her life while sitting in a hot dentist's waiting room, waiting for Aunt Florence. It took a lifetime before she wrote about the experience in one of her most famous poems, "In the Waiting Room," the moment when suddenly she realized she was both separate from and connected to everyone else:

The cover of the February 1918 issue of *National Geographic Magazine*, which Elizabeth read in a dentist's waiting room. Its exotic images triggered a disorienting reaction, one Elizabeth never forgot. She recalled the experience in her poem "In the Waiting Room," written in the 1970s when she was in her sixties.

> I said to myself: three days
> And you'll be seven years old.
> I was saying it to stop
> the sensation of falling off
> the round, turning world
> into cold, blue-black space.
> But I felt: You are an *I*,
> you are an *Elizabeth*,
> you are one of *them*.
> *Why* should you be one, too?
> …
> I knew nothing stranger
> had ever happened, that nothing
> stranger could ever happen.

In this poem the child and the poet were acutely aware that the war was on. Elizabeth was also engaged in her own inner war, which triggered serious illness. She described it in "The Country Mouse":

> First came constipation, then eczema again, and finally asthma. I felt myself aging, even dying. I was *bored* and lonely with Grandma, my silent grandpa, the dinners alone, bored with Emma and Beppo, all of them. At night I lay blinking my flashlight off and on, and crying.

ADOLESCENCE   49

Maude and George Shepherdson's home in Revere, Massachusetts

The SOS was finally heeded and a truce called in May 1918, when John Bishop took Elizabeth to Revere and Ronald carried her, too sick to walk, up the stairs to the apartment where Aunt Maude and Uncle George lived. The Bishops realized they had made a mistake and returned Elizabeth to her mother's family, though not immediately to Nova Scotia.

Maude and George Shepherdson were married in Great Village in April 1908 and later that year moved to Massachusetts. They lived on the top floor of a two-storey tenement house in Revere. Maude was a decidedly petite and gentle woman who was a gifted painter, like her uncle George Hutchinson, with whom she had studied in the 1890s. George Shepherdson was a marked contrast, exceptionally tall and stern. Elizabeth was never fond of George. However, even after Maude's death in 1940, Elizabeth and George remained connected for years and she was the beneficiary of his life insurance when he died in the 1960s.

Childless in 1918, the couple unhesitatingly opened their home to their ill niece. Elizabeth knew that they received money for her care—from her own estate—but she believed Maude would have taken her in even without this benefit. Elizabeth was also cared for during the next few years by Aunt Grace, who lived in Boston and worked as a nurse at the Massachusetts General and Boston Lying-In hospitals. Grace was a loving, practical, and

Elizabeth Bishop's aunt Maude Bulmer Shepherdson, *circa* 1880

funny woman. Elizabeth credited Grace with saving her life at this point, as this capable nurse, who was soon supervising staff, took Elizabeth's health care in hand and got her to the right doctors. Though she lived with and was devoted to Maude, it was Grace who became Elizabeth's favourite aunt. Since Grace lived until 1977, she was also the Bulmer with whom Elizabeth was longest and most lovingly connected.

Life in Revere during the late 1910s and early 1920s was a distinct contrast to life in Worcester. The Shepherdsons lived

Elizabeth Bishop's aunt Grace Bulmer Bowers, 1909

in a working-class neighbourhood, filled with Italian and Irish immigrants, people who fascinated Elizabeth. She remembered playing with the neighbourhood children, sitting with Aunt Maude at the piano singing songs when the housework needed to be done, and visiting their red-haired Irish neighbour Mrs. Sullivan, who was friendly and confiding. She wrote about this

The *North Star* aground in 1919. Owned by the Boston and Yarmouth Steamship Company, it and its sister ships were luxurious steamers with lounges, orchestras, restaurants, and two classes of cabins.

time and place in a memoir tentatively titled "Mrs. Sullivan Downstairs," but she never finished it.

It took over a year for Elizabeth to recover. Interestingly, as the great influenza epidemic of 1918 raged around her, Elizabeth's illness and confinement likely saved her weak lungs from succumbing to this disease. Her memories were of lying in bed wheezing from asthma and of Aunt Maude going out to get her more books. Once she was well enough, the Shepherdsons took her to art galleries and museums, enthusiasms they all shared. Then in the summer of 1919, she was able to go back to Nova Scotia. She went with Grace in early August aboard the steamer *North Star*, which ran between Boston and Yarmouth. As the ship approached the Nova Scotia coast in heavy fog and a high sea, it grounded on Green Island, and was stranded and seriously damaged. A major rescue operation ensued. The 270 passengers and several prize thoroughbred racehorses in

Listening to her grandfather read from the family Bible and looking at the thousands of images in that book was, arguably, the first way Elizabeth learned about faraway countries, which sparked her imagination and desire to travel. The Bulmer family Bible became the source for her poem "Over 2,000 Illustrations and a Complete Concordance," published in *Poems: North & South / A Cold Spring* in 1955, the book which won the Pulitzer Prize in 1956.

the hold were safely removed. Grace and Elizabeth continued on their way to Great Village by train the next day, passing through Halifax, which was still visibly shattered from the Halifax Explosion.

This trip marked a return to what Elizabeth knew and loved best, her maternal grandparents' home; but she never again lived permanently in Great Village. Increasingly, it was clear that her mother would not recover. Her grandparents were getting older, and her aunts were better able to raise her. Massachusetts indeed offered more educational opportunity, so again the adults in her life decided it was best for Elizabeth to live mainly in the United States with Maude and George. What the 1919 trip began was a decade of migration back and forth between Nova Scotia and New England, first accompanied by her aunts, and then, as she grew old enough, travelling on her own.

Where is the artist in all this life? Elizabeth learned to read and write in Great Village. She had vivid memories of making letters and numbers on her school slate, their meanings mysterious to her though their shapes held aesthetic pleasure. She told friends that she first became aware of the power of language through two people: Gammie and Dr. T. R. Johnson, both of whom had delighted and surprised her with rhymes.

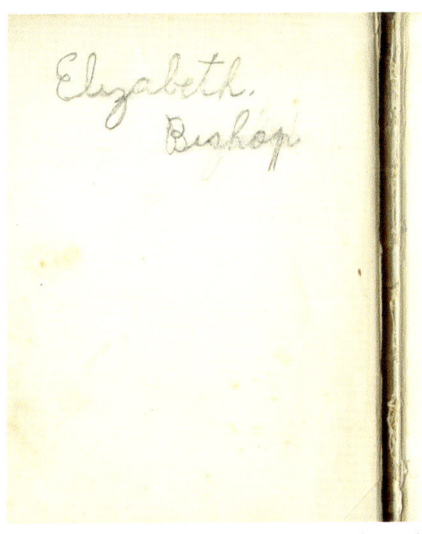

A CHILD'S GARDEN OF VERSES

Elizabeth Bishop's signature on the title page of her copy of Robert Louis Stevenson's *A Child's Garden of Verses*

Their spoken words, part of the vibrant oral tradition of Nova Scotia's culture, impressed her curious mind. She remembered listening to Pa read quietly to the family from Robert Burns or the Bible in the parlour after tea. Her mother and aunts had belonged to the Christophian Literary Society, and throughout her childhood Maude and Grace recited Browning and Tennyson to her. They actively encouraged her own reading of poetry. One of her prized books, bearing her signature, was Robert Louis Stevenson's *A Child's Garden of Verses*. She remembered she began writing poetry when she was eight years old, that is, in 1919—perhaps during that first summer back in Great Village.

Great Village was a multi-sensory place: sights, sounds, scents, textures, and flavours abounded and Elizabeth's

Elizabeth Bishop, *circa* 1920–1921

The earliest known correspondence by Elizabeth Bishop, a postcard she sent to Aunt Maude from Camp Chequessett in Massachusetts, July 1928

precocious mind absorbed everything and learned how to see, hear, smell, touch, and taste the world. It was also the place of her greatest sorrow: the breakdown, disappearance, and hospitalization of her mother, a kind of living death. In June 1915, only weeks after Gertrude and Elizabeth first returned to Great Village, Frank Elwood, the two-month-old son of Arthur and Mabel Bulmer, died. Decades later, Elizabeth wrote about this sad event in "First Death in Nova Scotia." In 1922, during one of her long summer visits, her friend Gwendolyn Patriquin, a diabetic, died. Again, decades later, Elizabeth wrote a powerful memoir, "Gwendolyn," about this child and her own sense of guilt around her death.

Ultimately, Great Village was the place where life and death, love and loss, existed most closely together. Throughout her life, Elizabeth carried these conditions—a "sweet / sensation of joy," connected to the vibrant sensory world of Great Village, and "an immense sibilant, glistening loneliness," connected to her too-early acquaintance with death, grief, and guilt—wherever she went. Great Village was her principal site of awe. For the young artist, this place and time and these people (Great Village during her childhood with her maternal family) profoundly affected her artistic sensibility.

Adolescence is a turbulent time for all of us as we struggle to form our mature identities. Elizabeth took into her teenage years more experience than many people amass in a lifetime. She continued to live with Maude and George, but, increasingly, she established an independent path. As her health improved, she received her first sustained formal education. She attended junior high in Revere in 1924–1925. When the Shepherdsons moved to Saugus, Massachusetts, Elizabeth attended Saugus High School in 1925–1926. In 1926–1927 she went to North Shore Country Day School in Swampscott, where she published her writing in the *Owl*, the school magazine, her first publication. For several years, she also attended Camp Chequessett on Cape Cod, a nautical summer camp where she learned to sail. Her visits to Great Village continued right up until 1930, the year she entered Vassar College.

Elizabeth was a good student who maintained high marks. Her ability prompted the Bishops to urge preparatory school for college. In the fall of 1927 she was enrolled at Walnut Hill, a private boarding school in Natick, Massachusetts, which she attended until she graduated in 1930. Elizabeth's own estate paid for her education. She also received money from a trust fund set up by her paternal grandfather. John and Sarah Bishop died within five days of each other in 1925, leaving Uncle Jack in control of her finances.

When Jack arranged for Elizabeth to go to Walnut Hill, he told the assistant principal, Harriet Farwell, that his niece knew nothing about her ill mother. Much to Farwell's credit, she realized that Elizabeth in fact knew a great deal about her mother, and that it made her sad and affected her behaviour.

ADOLESCENCE

The Blue Pencil

Elizabeth attended Walnut Hill School from 1927–1930. She published her poetry and prose in the *Blue Pencil* and served as book review editor and in her senior year as editor. The magazine was a major production, appearing four times a year, each issue running to fifty pages. It reported on all manner of school activities, but a significant portion was devoted to creative and critical writing.

The understanding and support Elizabeth received at Walnut Hill helped this brilliant, troubled young woman and artist cope with increasing independence and alienation, as she navigated the rigours of adolescence.

Elizabeth also regularly published poetry and prose in the *Blue Pencil*, the Walnut Hill School magazine. So identified was she in the minds of her peers with the literary arts and her childhood home, that her senior class prophecy foretold: "Miss Bishop, the poet laureate of Nova Scotia. Walnut Hill has proudly placed her bust in the alcove, while she remains in Nova Scotian seclusion."

It was at Walnut Hill where Elizabeth's independence and particular path was most directly fostered and advanced. There she met a number of young women who became lifelong friends, including Frani Blough, Joan Collingwood, Barbara Chesney, and Margaret Mann. As unsettled and troubled as Elizabeth was, she worked to establish not only her identity but also a community of her own. In adolescence the tendency is to do so in opposition to one's family. It was at this time that Elizabeth began to call her friends her family. She needed to separate herself from a painful, complex past. However, as we usually discover, while it is important to become ourselves, to know who we are as individuals, we are always intimately linked to where we came from and what we have known.

During Elizabeth's senior year of high school, she visited

Great Village over the Christmas holiday of 1929–1930. It was the last time she saw her beloved Pa. He died in February. It was also her last visit to Nova Scotia for sixteen years. When she graduated from Walnut Hill in the spring of 1930 and made plans to enter Vassar College in the fall, Elizabeth was at a turning point in her life. She stood facing the unknown future, a new path that would take her far away in time and space from her childhood home and her mother's family. Though plagued by self-doubt then and for much of her life, even at this early age Elizabeth knew what she wanted from her art: a way to explore, express, and understand the mysteries and contradictions of home and travel, love and loss, life and death.

Elizabeth Bishop's photo from the *Vassarian*, the Vassar College yearbook in 1934, her graduating year

CHAPTER FIVE

"LONG LEAGUES OF THEE..."
VASSAR, EUROPE, & EARLY PUBLICATIONS

Not long after William Bulmer's death, Elizabeth's grandmother Elizabeth Bulmer became ill and was cared for by her youngest daughter, Mary Ross, a nurse, who was married and lived in Montreal. Elizabeth visited Gammie with Maude and George in the summer of 1930; it was the last time she saw her before her death in April 1931. Grace was back in Great Village, married to William Bowers and raising her own family on a large, prosperous farm called Elmcroft, which became an important site for Elizabeth in the 1940s. But at this point in the early 1930s, Elizabeth's ties with her childhood home were suspended. Her mother was still alive, but with the passing years, with no Gammie or Pa to hold out hope, with her life stretching out before her, this living death was a burden she wanted to drop. Sadly, her effort to do so only caused more pain and guilt.

Elizabeth spent much of her childhood avoiding direct reference to her mother. The Bishops were silent about Gertrude. The Bulmers grieved and tried to carry on. She learned early to hide her thoughts and feelings from the adults around her, and she turned more and more towards poetry (and art generally) to divert her from what she described, in her adolescent poem "To a Tree," as "my tiny tragedies and grotesque grieves." She believed art could heal. In a 1928 poem, she wrote:

> Oh, for the healing swaying, old and low,
> Of some song sung to rest the tired dead,
> A song to fall like water on my head,
> And over quivering limbs, dream flushed to glow!

> There is magic made by melody:
> A spell of rest, and quiet breath, and cool
> Heart, that sinks through fading colours deep
> To the subaqueous stillness of the sea,
> And floats forever in a moon-green pool,
> Held in the arms of rhythm and of sleep.

However, everywhere in poetry she found that imagination was mixed up with her life. Life and art haunted each other. As hard as she tried to maintain solitude and independence, the deeper inside her art she went, the more directly she had to grapple with the troubles in her life.

In one of her Walnut Hill essays, "In Appreciation of Shelley's Poems," written in 1927, she declared, "The only real way to understand poetry is to know the life and beliefs of the poet." This view was no adolescent naïvety. In a 1964 letter to Grace, she wrote: "I like to know about he lives of writers I read, don't you?" Adding, "It helps to understand my poetry if the reader knows something of my life." She advocated reading biographies in tandem with the work in order to see the way life and art connected.

Sailing one day off Cape Cod in the 1920s, she camped overnight on an island. All she had with her was Shelley's poetry. The effect of reading his work as the sun rose the next day was unforgettable. For Elizabeth, "Shelley was a spirit of the sunrise." Art was part of the elemental nature of the world. She had learned this from her mother in Great Village.

Elizabeth had also discovered the work of Hopkins. His epic poem "The Wreck of the Deutschland" profoundly affected her. It spoke to her directly about her mother. On the deck of the sinking ship a nun named Gertrude stands crying out to Christ as a storm shatters her world. For Elizabeth, her mother was both the victim and the storm (that is, effect and cause). Reading poetry during her adolescence, Elizabeth learned that art was a source of both solace and challenge, of escape and confrontation. Art led her away from and back to her mother and their shipwrecked love.

In the fall of 1930 Elizabeth left the familiarity and continuity of high school, where she had been understood and supported, and entered the more competitive realm of Vassar College, where she was only one more freshman. After a rocky first year—at one point she and a friend ran away—Elizabeth settled down, immersed herself in her studies, and gradually established her own little society of like-minded friends.

Vassar College, Poughkeepsie, New York

She first concentrated on music, but because public performance, which frightened her, was required, she abandoned it for literature. She was also fascinated by science, and thought about becoming a doctor—an idea she carried into the 1940s when, discouraged by her lack of literary progress, she considered abandoning writing entirely for medicine. By her junior year she was immersed in the literary realm and had made a reputation for herself as an intellectual. One of her English teachers knew early on that Elizabeth was "doomed to be a poet" and that she was entirely capable of attending to her own education.

She was involved with the Vassar literary publications, but because they were stuffy and formal, she and several classmates also founded their own more radical journal, *Con Spirito*. She was involved in theatrical productions. She interviewed T. S. Eliot. She became editor-in-chief of the *Vassarian*, her graduation

VASSAR, EUROPE, & EARLY PUBLICATIONS

Vassar College

Vassar College was founded by businessman, philanthropist, and women's education advocate Matthew Vassar in 1861. It was still an all-women's college when Elizabeth Bishop attended from 1930–1934, but it is now a co-educational institution. In 2011, Vassar celebrates its 150th anniversary, the same year as Elizabeth's centenary.

yearbook. She also began publishing poems in literary journals outside of school. Her future path seemed to be taking shape.

This time (1930–1934) was the cusp between adolescence and adulthood, with the latter pulling ever more strongly, demanding she decide what to do with her life. School gave her structure, rhythm, purpose; but all her efforts were directed towards leaving behind this regularity. When she graduated in 1934, Elizabeth told Frani Blough that it felt like she was standing at the end of a diving board not able to jump or go back, a strange in-between state. Indecision was to be a perennial condition for Elizabeth throughout her life.

A more negative activity that came out of these years was drinking. The United States was in the throes of prohibition, and Elizabeth and her friends discovered the illicit pleasures of the illegal speakeasies of Poughkeepsie, and later, New York City. The culture drew her into this activity, but, unfortunately, her temperament made what is often a passing phase of youthful experimenting into a permanent condition: alcoholism. She struggled with it for the rest of her life.

As an adult, after years of therapy and attempts to control her drinking, she identified an inheritance from both sides of her family: John Bishop, Jack Bishop, Arthur Bulmer, and even her father had problems with alcohol. She also acknowledged the emotional traumas that affected her ability to cope with addiction and located them in her relationship with her mother. Gertrude never touched alcohol, but for Elizabeth, the sense of abandonment she felt when her mother vanished, the fact that she felt responsible for it in some way, intensified her guilt, shame, sorrow, and desire to escape.

Elizabeth's emerging sexuality was also making itself felt at this time. While she had a brief serious relationship with a young man, Robert Seaver, during her senior year at Vassar, Elizabeth's closest friends were young women. Throughout her life, she had several abiding and passionate friendships with men (her relationship with Robert Lowell, for example, lasted thirty years), but her most intimate relationships were with women.

During the early 1930s, Elizabeth began to realize not only her preference—that she loved women—but also the fact that it came with complications. The wider cultural and political climate not only disapproved of lesbianism and homosexuality, but actually criminalized them and defined them as immoral, a situation that forced many men and women to conceal this part of their lives. Even as society's views slowly began to change in the 1970s, by her own admission, Elizabeth always preferred "closets, closets, and more closets." In spite of these brutal taboos, during the 1930s and 1940s Elizabeth had significant relationships with Margaret Miller, Louise Crane, and Marjorie Stevens.

Gertrude Bishop died on May 29, 1934, just before her daughter graduated from college. The only direct comment that survives from Elizabeth about this event was made to Frani: "I guess I should tell you that mother died a week ago today. After eighteen years of course it is the happiest thing that could have happened." This matter-of-fact brevity masks the profound impact of death's finality and grief's ravages, described in a 1935 poem, "The Reprimand":

> To only eyes; their deepest sorrow they wrung
> From water. Where wept water's gone
> That residue is sorrow, salt and wan,
> Your bitter enemy, who leaves the face white-strung.

VASSAR, EUROPE, & EARLY PUBLICATIONS

Elizabeth (front row, middle), pictured with the other members of the *Vassarian* yearbook committee in 1934

Elizabeth had already met the well-known poet Marianne Moore, who immediately took the fledgling writer under her wing and helped get her work published. Moore introduced her protegé in *Trial Balances* (1935), an anthology of what today would be called emerging writers. Elizabeth was intrigued by the single Moore's close relationship with her elderly mother. Moore was fatherless, too. Her father had suffered from mental illness and been hospitalized when Moore was a child. Though Elizabeth eventually left Moore's literary nest as a result of a disagreement over Elizabeth's war poem "Roosters" (though the independent Elizabeth would not have stayed long under anyone's literary influence), they remained good friends until Moore's death in 1972.

What began when Elizabeth left Vassar was a decade of restless travel, with a slow progression towards the publication of her first collection of poetry and a belated return to Nova Scotia, both in 1946. World travel had taken hold of Elizabeth while she was still in school. In 1932, she and her classmate Evelyn Huntington went to Newfoundland (not yet a part of Canada) and did a walking tour of the Avalon Peninsula. Its remoteness, its unlikeliness as a destination, and the fact that Great-Uncle George had painted it, motivated Elizabeth's choice for her first real trip off the continent. She and Evelyn travelled by freighter, Elizabeth's preferred mode of transportation for the rest of her life.

In 1934 Elizabeth moved to New York, where she would live periodically for the next ten years; but almost immediately she decamped for Europe, where she spent much of the next three years (1935–1937) travelling and living at times on her own or with Louise Crane. Europe was not only an immersion in high art and culture, but also an explosion of sensory experiences. A number of poems came out of this time, including "A Miracle for Breakfast," "Quai d'Orleans," "Sleeping on the Ceiling," and "Paris, 7 A.M."

As desperate as she was to move far away from her past, while on board the German freighter *Königstein* in 1935, slipping further out to sea, Elizabeth suffered a bout of severe disorientation:

> I have been overtaken by an awful, awful feeling of deathly physical and mental <u>illness</u>—something seems 'after' me. It is as if one were whirled off from all the world…in a sort of cloud—dark, sulphurous…grey, of melancholia.

She identified this state (remarkably like the one she had felt in the dentist's waiting room in February 1918) as homesickness. It was accompanied by a new round of physical illness as her asthma and allergies intensified and her drinking increased. She was once again adrift, and her body and mind reacted, often necessitating hospitalization.

Fresh sorrows also continued. During the 1937 trip to Europe, she, Louise Crane, and Margaret Miller were involved in a car accident which resulted in a terrible injury to Miller, an aspiring painter: the amputation of her right arm below the elbow. This tragedy not only profoundly altered Miller's life, but also deeply affected Elizabeth, who was haunted by the accident for years, adding to her already large store of guilt.

Elizabeth Bishop (right) and Louise Crane, New York City, late 1930s

In December 1937, Elizabeth returned to the United States. Uncomfortable living in New York for any length of time, early in 1938 she went to Key West, Florida, where she set up housekeeping with Louise. Preferring the warmer climate and wanting to be near Elizabeth, Aunt Maude and Uncle George also moved there, and lived nearby. Trips back north were relatively frequent and usually unpleasant, so for the next decade the south was Elizabeth's main base. In Key West she wrote many of the poems that made up her first book. The rural vibrancy of pre-war Florida, the warm, humid climate, and the leisurely way of life appealed to Elizabeth. She felt liberated, and for a while was productive. Then, in 1940, Maude left her canary with Elizabeth and drove all the way to Great Village, where on August 7 she died. Elizabeth's losses kept mounting.

Elizabeth met Marjorie Stevens in the spring of 1941. Their relationship was central in Elizabeth's life for the next six years.

Left to right: George Shepherdson, Louise Crane, Elizabeth Bishop, Maude Shepherdson, and unidentified man in Key West, Florida

They travelled together to Mexico and Nova Scotia, but eventually went their separate ways, though they always remained friends. An unfinished poem from this time, "It is marvellous to wake up together," spoke about the power of passion and the fragility of love:

> It is marvellous to wake up together
> At the same minute: marvellous to hear
> The rain begin suddenly all over the roof,
> To feel the air suddenly clear
>   ....Without surprise
> The world might change to something quite different,
> As the air changes or the lightning comes without our blinking,
> Change as our kisses are changing without our thinking.

   For Elizabeth, love was inextricably linked to loss. Indeed, love and loss defined each other.
   While in New York in the fall of 1941, Elizabeth met Lota de Macedo Soares. Though nothing came of that meeting at the time, ten years later their reconnection in Brazil gave Elizabeth the most important relationship of her adult life and over a

Trial Balances was Elizabeth's first publication in a book. This anthology, edited by Ann Winslow and published in 1936, was premised on the idea of a senior, established poet introducing an up-and-coming younger poet. Marianne Moore introduced Elizabeth Bishop.

decade of happiness and stability, which allowed her to solidify a remarkable literary legacy. But for now, the early 1940s, Key West remained her home.

With the outbreak of World War II in 1939, Key West began a major transformation as the American navy expanded its base and became a dominant presence. Elizabeth tried to adjust to this shift and even took a job at the naval yard grinding lenses for binoculars. But the work made her sick, and the war's intrusion was unsettling. The town became even more unpleasant than New York and she began to go north more frequently, growing restless again. She described herself to Moore as "the grasshopper-type girl." She was often quite ill during this time, especially in 1943–1944, when she struggled with regular, debilitating asthma attacks, exacerbated by bouts of heavy drinking.

In May 1945 she learned that she had received the Houghton Mifflin Poetry Award, which provided prize money and the publication of her first book, *North & South*. This positive development actually triggered a crisis severe enough that Elizabeth sought therapy from a couple of doctors. Her good intentions to move forward, her efforts to find a place to live and call home (she and Louise bought a house in Key West, which they owned until 1946), her determination to hold onto love and companionship, to write and be productive, were unravelling, if they had ever really fused. The weight of loss and grief was immense.

She had spent the past decade ignoring or pushing aside the past. She realized that on the eve of the publication of her first major artistic expression, in order to accept its existence and continue writing, she had to confront her past directly,

Maude and George Shepherdson, Key West, Florida, 1937

not run away from it; she had to remember her childhood, not forget it; she had to return to Nova Scotia and reclaim for her art what Brett Millier, Elizabeth's first biographer, calls her motherland. Perhaps none of these ideas were fully formed in Elizabeth's mind, though her letters from this time, especially to Moore, reveal her struggle: "I feel I *must* do something about my Life & Works very soon—this wastefulness is a sin—but I just can't figure out what. I wish it were 1934 all over again. I'd do everything quite differently." This pessimism sat right beside giddiness as she then told Moore of her plan to attend a Ringling Brothers Circus show (she and Moore shared a love of the circus) the next time she went to Miami for a dentist's appointment.

Elizabeth Bishop's long-time partner Lota de Macedo Soares with Sammy the toucan, Samambaia, Brazil

CHAPTER SIX

"DRIVING TO THE INTERIOR…"
THE BRAZIL YEARS

IN EARLY July 1946, Elizabeth Bishop abruptly left New York and travelled to Halifax. She stayed for a couple of weeks at the Nova Scotian Hotel near the city's waterfront. Mount Hope was almost directly across the harbour. Elizabeth could not have confronted her past more literally. She saw Zilpha Linkletter, a friend in the city whom she had met through Ella and Bligh DesBrisay, childhood friends from Great Village who lived in New York. She asked Zilpha, a government bureaucrat, how to locate medical information about her mother. Zilpha advised her but never asked Elizabeth if she succeeded. No direct evidence exists to confirm her success, but it is likely that she went to the hospital and saw her mother's records.

Elizabeth then went to Lockeport on the South Shore, where she stayed for about a month. Finally, she returned to Great Village and stayed with Grace at Elmcroft (her grandparents' home now belonged to one of Grace's stepsons). Her intention was to remain until the end of the summer, but business required her presence in the United States and one afternoon in late August she boarded a bus in front of the farm and went back to

Elmcroft Farm, Great Village, Nova Scotia

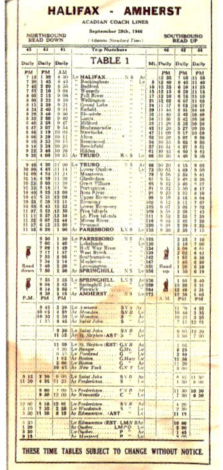

Boston. Decades later, this moment anchored one of her most masterful poems, "The Moose."

This first visit to Nova Scotia in sixteen years, this confrontation with her past, gave back her memories and allowed her to begin writing more directly about her childhood home. Most immediately from this visit came the poem "At the Fishhouses," with its startling image of total immersion and haunting evocations of the subconscious as sea, and its description of knowledge as a bitter, briny flame that burns the tongue. In it, Elizabeth acknowledged that we are elementally, forever part of history, whatever it might be:

The 1946 Acadian Lines schedule, from around the time Elizabeth travelled to Boston from Great Village

> It is like what we imagine knowledge to be:
> dark, salt, clear, moving, utterly free,
> Drawn from the cold hard mouth
> of the world, derived from the rocky breasts
> forever, flowing and drawn, and since
> our knowledge is historical, flowing, and flown.

Now that she had returned, Elizabeth made another trip to Nova Scotia in 1947, this time with Marjorie Stevens. They stayed for some weeks in Breton Cove on Cape Breton Island. From that time came the poem "Cape Breton." She chose the island for several reasons, including the fact that as a young woman Gertrude had taught school there. Elizabeth was actively in search of her mother's life, trying to understand what

The Pulitzer Prize

The Pulitzer Prize was established in honour of the Hungarian-American journalist and publisher Joseph Pulitzer, who died in 1911, the year Elizabeth was born. The first Pulitzer prizes were awarded in 1917. The prizes are given out in twenty-one categories, for excellence in newspaper journalism, literary achievements, and musical composition.

had happened to her. Another poem from this time, "Insomnia," speaks about their relationship and Elizabeth's realization that Gertrude had been deserted by the universe, abandoned in a well (another water metaphor about the subconscious) where their love had been turned upside down.

Elizabeth and Marjorie also stayed in Great Village for a few weeks—Marjorie and Grace became good friends. More time on the Bowers farm produced Elizabeth's intriguing poem "The Prodigal." Like her prodigal, it took Elizabeth "a long time / finally to make up [her] mind to go home"; but when she did, after a decade of restlessness and illness, she discovered that time had given her courage to confront the shuddering insights of memory.

The poems she wrote in the late 1940s became *A Cold Spring*, which, combined with those from *North & South*, were published as *Poems* in 1955, when she had already been in Brazil for several years. This collection received the Pulitzer Prize for Poetry in 1956.

Elizabeth's return to Nova Scotia coincided with another important event. In January 1947, the poet and critic Randall Jarrell introduced her to the poet Robert Lowell. The thirty-year friendship between these two very different artists was one of the most sustained and complex of both their lives. Lowell became a celebrity, a giant personality among contemporary writers. His admiration of and devotion to Elizabeth (even amid the tumult of his manic depression, political views, and shifting relationships) was unwavering. His influence, especially in the late

From the *Estudio*

Shortly after Elizabeth arrived in Brazil, its vibrant sights and sounds and its expressive people began to inspire poems and stories. Elizabeth worried that being an outsider meant she had no right to describe or comment on life in Brazil, but her natural curiosity and empathy compelled her to create art from her Brazilian experiences. Some of Elizabeth Bishop's Brazilian poems include:

"Arrival at Santos"
"Brazil, January 1, 1502"
"Questions of Travel"
"Squatter's Children"
"Manuelzinho"
"The Armadillo"
"The Riverman"
"The Burglar of Babylon"
"Pink Dog"
"Santarém"

Her Brazilian stories include:

"A Trip to Vigia"
"To the Botequim and Back"

1940s and early 1950s, brought her financial support and professional recognition, which she always appreciated but which also sometimes made her uncomfortable.

Even as her return to Nova Scotia got her writing again, Elizabeth still struggled with daily life. She continued to move back and forth between Florida and New York, and added Maine to her places of refuge. (Maine reminded her of Nova Scotia, and it became especially important to her in the 1970s.) An encounter with Lowell there in 1948, when he may or may not have proposed marriage, unsettled her. Her close time with Marjorie was over. Her relationship with another old, close friend, Tom Wanning, was shifting. The lack of a serious connection set her adrift again. She was drinking too much, and was frequently sick and struggling with depression. Gradually it dawned on Elizabeth that a major change was needed. However, the vice of indecision was tight.

Lowell intervened and helped to secure the post of the Poetry Consultant to the Library of Congress (now called Poet Laureate) for her for the term September 1949 to September 1950. This highly public position terrified the shy Elizabeth.

She resisted, but eventually agreed, even though she felt like a fraud, with only one slim volume to her name. Before heading to Washington, D.C., Elizabeth spent time at Yaddo, an artists' colony in Saratoga Springs, New York. Again, Lowell helped to arrange it. She returned in the fall and winter of 1950–1951. Though she did not much like Yaddo, while there she met several people who became dear, lifelong friends: the poet May Swenson, the painter Kit Barker, and his wife, the novelist Ilse Barker.

Elizabeth's time in Washington was dismal, and she was often sick. She frequently retreated to the Maryland farm owned by her old friend Jane Dewey, a physicist. Dewey was the daughter of the philosopher John Dewey, who had a summer home in Nova Scotia. He and Jane had also spent time in Florida when Elizabeth lived there. By March 1951, when she left Yaddo for the second time, Elizabeth had decided she could no longer delay the major change. She turned to the old choice: travel. She decided to take a sea voyage around the world. Before embarking on this archetypal journey, she returned once more to Nova Scotia. Her specific destination was Sable Island, 160 kilometres off the coast, a large sandbar perched on the edge of the continental shelf.

Pansy, the Bowers family's Sable Island horse

Ouro Prêto, Brazil

According to Bulmer family oral tradition, Elizabeth's great-grandfather Robert Hutchinson was shipwrecked there in the mid-1860s. As she told Lowell, "If I am not fulfilling my destiny and get wrecked, too, I think I can turn it into an article and maybe a poem or two." She wanted to see the island's famous horses (Aunt Grace owned one of them, which Elizabeth had met in 1946) and the Ipswich sparrow, Sable Island being their only nesting site.

She pitched a story about the island to *The New Yorker* and started it immediately after her visit. Tentatively titled "The Deadly Sandpile," it was never finished. Standing on the windswept dunes so far out in the Atlantic, at such a turning point in her life, Elizabeth linked the island to one of the most distinctive lingual expressions of her childhood home, the indrawn yes—which found its way into "The Moose" years later:

"Yes…" that peculiar
affirmative. "Yes…"
A sharp indrawn breath,
half groan, half acceptance,
that means "Life's like that.
We know *it* (also death)."

On November 10, 1951, Elizabeth boarded the SS *Bowplate* in New York and began her journey south. While at sea, she contemplated the unbroken horizon and wondered what she would find when she reached her destination. What was her destination? She resolved to be more positive about the future and wrote in her journal that she believed "love will unexpectedly appear over & over again…that people will continue to do deeds that astound me."

This commitment and belief manifested almost immediately when she made landfall in Brazil over two weeks later. She

The *Bowplate*

In November 1951, Elizabeth boarded the *Bowplate* in New York, intending to travel around the world. The *Bowplate* was built in 1944 and bought by Norwegian shipowners Rederiet Odfjell in 1947. Its regular route was from New York to Santos to Buenos Aires and around Cape Horn (the southernmost tip of South America). It often transported coffee. Elizabeth's great-grandfather Robert Hutchinson had sailed around Cape Horn in the nineteenth century and she was conscious of following in his footsteps.

intended to visit her friends Mary Morse, Pearl Kazin, and Lota de Macedo Soares for only a few weeks. In mid-December she had a terrible allergic reaction to the fruit of the cashew, which required hospitalization and a significant recovery time. Lota took her into her apartment in Rio de Janeiro and nursed her back to health. Still in Brazil in February 1952, Elizabeth was astonished to receive a toucan for her forty-first birthday.

By this time Lota and Elizabeth had decided to live together. For the first time in her adult life, holding onto her resolution to believe, Elizabeth found a real home in the most unexpected place. Brazil was her home for the next fifteen years.

Lota was a lively, smart, expressive, extroverted woman. She came from a prominent Rio family and immediately introduced Elizabeth to the Brazilian intelligentsia. Lota was passionate about art and architecture, and was designing and building an ultra-modern house near Petrópolis, at a place called Samambaia. One of the first things she did for Elizabeth was build her an *estudio*, her own place to write, which so overwhelmed Elizabeth that she told Pearl, "I'm sure I'll just sit in it weeping with joy for weeks and not write a line."

Elizabeth was, however, writing well. The next decade was arguably the most productive of her life. Almost instantly, and to her surprise, she was writing poems and stories about her childhood, work which was openly autobiographical, including

The view from Elizabeth Bishop's studio in Samambaia, as it is today

her most important artistic statement about her relationship with her mother, "In the Village."

The vibrant life of rural Brazil acted as a trigger and catalyst for remembering. But even more than the environment, Lota's love, good sense, respect, and support—the stability of their relationship—freed Elizabeth in unprecedented ways. The home they made for themselves was filled with birds and animals, with children (those of their maid and those of Lota's adopted son), art, books, music, evolving gardens, regular gatherings of friends that entailed much cooking—just like it was in Gammie and Pa's home. They travelled to Ouro Prêto, a well-preserved eighteenth-century colonial city. Elizabeth loved it and the other small cities in Minas Gerais. Years later, in more difficult times, she bought a dilapidated eighteenth-century house perched high on a hillside above Ouro Prêto and restored it. It was the first home she owned alone (the Key West house had been shared with Louise).

Elizabeth was also writing about Brazil. Over the next decade significant Brazilian poems and stories emerged. After be-

Elizabeth's early years in Brazil were a productive time not only for writing but also for painting. From childhood, Elizabeth was surrounded by paintings and painters. Her grandparents' home was filled with paintings by George Hutchinson and Maude Shepherdson. Elizabeth herself began to paint at an early age and retained a lifelong fascination with visual art. In the mid-1990s William Benton collected the known works of Elizabeth and published them in a book called *Exchanging Hats*. A number of her posthumously published collections and books about her use her art on the covers.

ing published in literary journals and magazines, especially *The New Yorker*, this Brazilian and the Nova Scotian work appeared in *Questions of Travel* in 1965. In the early 1950s, Elizabeth was still shepherding *Poems: North & South/A Cold Spring* to publication. Finally, in 1955, it appeared. She was excited about receiving the Pulitzer Prize in 1956 mostly because it showed Lota's family and friends that she was, in fact, a real poet.

Lota introduced Elizabeth to *Mina Vida de Menina*, a classic of Brazilian literature. It was a diary written in the late 1890s by a little girl, "Helena Morley" (a pseudonym), who lived in Diamantina. Though she knew no Portuguese,

Elizabeth decided to translate it and get it published in the United States (a project not unlike her great-uncle John Robert Hutchinson's translation of the Indian novel *Fortune's Wheel*). This work took several years, during which Elizabeth met the elderly "Helena," whose real name was Senhora Augusto Mario Caldeira Brant, and travelled to Diamantina. *The Diary of 'Helena Morley'* was published in 1957. Elizabeth also translated Henrique Mindlin's *Modern Architecture in Brazil* (1956), and throughout the 1950s and 1960s translated works by other Brazilian writers, including Joaquim Cardozo, Carlos Drummond de Andrade, and Clarice Lispector. In the early 1970s she co-edited with Emanuel Brasil an *Anthology of Twentieth-Century Brazilian Poetry* (1972).

The 1950s was a leisurely but highly productive time for Elizabeth and Lota. They spent most of it at Samambaia, up in the mountains, as the big modern house was completed, going into Rio only when necessary. There were also some trips around Brazil and to the United States, but for the most part Elizabeth was happily settled. Asthma, allergies, and alcohol still presented problems, but she coped relatively well. As 1960 arrived and a new decade dawned, her hope was for more of the same. It began wonderfully enough in February when she took a long-anticipated trip down the Amazon River.

The first hint that life was about to change came when Lota's old friend Carlos Lacerda was elected governor of the state of Guanabara. Lota approached him with the idea that an undeveloped landfill along the Rio coast be converted into a city park (Parque do Flamengo) and that she head the project. Lacerda agreed and the feisty, determined Lota was made "chief coordinatress." She was thrown into a whirlwind. Brazilian politics were chaotic and the government prone to coups, the economic climate was dismal and subject to rampant inflation, and the fact that a woman was in charge of such a massive construction project caused continuous conflicts, delays, and frustrations.

Casa Mariana, the house Elizabeth purchased and restored in Ouro Prêto, Brazil, as it is today

In terms of their life, Lota was now required to be almost always in Rio, a city Elizabeth disliked (the fact was, she did not like living in any city for very long). The demands of Lota's new job and her growing obsession with Brazilian politics and completing the park regardless of the obstacles caused strain and distress between them.

Elizabeth tried to distract herself by accepting a Time-Life project, a book about Brazil for their World Library series. It necessitated a trip to New York late in 1961. The editorial experience was so negative, however, that she came away discouraged and angry. She disowned the book when it appeared in 1962.

Anne Stevenson contacted Elizabeth in 1963 to ask if they could correspond. Stevenson was writing the first book about Elizabeth. Upset by Lota's preoccupations and feeling homesick for the north, Elizabeth was open to the kind of inquiry Stevenson proposed. A remarkable exchange of letters followed in 1964–1965, in which Elizabeth wrote candidly about her childhood and poetic process. Stevenson had hit the motherlode, so to speak. Her *Elizabeth Bishop* appeared in 1966.

By the mid-1960s, however, Lota's health began to deteriorate as a result of overwork and what was eventually diagnosed as arteriosclerosis. Elizabeth's health was also poor and she struggled with regular bouts of drinking, which caused conflict with Lota, who disapproved. Both became so sick in 1965 that they required hospitalization. Elizabeth decided to accept a teaching position at the University of Washington in Seattle for the first half of 1966. To reassure Lota that she was coming back, she bought a house in Ouro Prêto and began its restoration.

The plaque now affixed to Casa Mariana. Elizabeth named the house in honour of her early mentor, the poet Marianne Moore

The whole idea of teaching writing made Elizabeth uncomfortable and her self-doubt kicked in, causing loneliness and depression. While in Seattle, she had an affair with a young woman, which Lota found out about. When Elizabeth returned to Brazil, Lota's health was much worse. Their efforts to be together in late 1966 and early 1967 were painful, though neither wanted to give up. In the summer of 1967, Lota's doctor told Elizabeth to leave for a while. She went to New York. The plan was for Lota to join her there for a vacation when Lota was better, but Lota knew that she would not get better. Against the advice of her doctor, family, and friends, Lota flew to New York on September 19, 1967. That night, after spending a quiet evening with Elizabeth, Lota took an overdose of Valium, slipped into a coma, and died five days later at St. Vincent's Hospital.

Bulmer family home (right), the blacksmith shop (centre), the Great Village River bridge, *circa* 1916

CHAPTER SEVEN

"NATURE REPEATS HERSELF..."

RETURNING TO THE NORTH

Reeling from the devastating loss of Lota, after such a painful year trying to hold things together and hoping that somehow they would recover their life, Elizabeth Bishop turned to her friends in the dark months that closed 1967. Her letters are filled with an obsessive replay of events, repeated questions asking why it had happened, direct appeals to her friends not to abandon her, and aching affirmations of her love for Lota.

On Lota's will, which was read in October 1967, in her hand, was written: "Si le Bon Dieu exist, il me pardonnera. C'est son metier." (If God exists, he will forgive me. That's his job.) Elizabeth believed this indicated that Lota had intended to kill herself and that, at the end, what she wanted was to be with Elizabeth when she died. But suicide is also a most violent act. The fresh guilt this tragedy brought to Elizabeth remained with her for the rest of her life.

Lota's circumstances were uncannily similar to Gertrude's: a vibrant, restless, beautiful woman with an underlying, progressive medical condition (hyperthyroidism in Gertrude, arteriosclerosis in Lota); overburdened by stress and worry (custody and estate issues for Gertrude, the Rio park and politics for Lota); holding beliefs out of place in her milieu (Gertrude's suffragism and anti-war feelings, Lota's conviction that a woman could wield power), combined to undermine their mental stability. Both became erratic and acted out. Both were hospitalized and received what was thought to be the best possible modern care for the time, which utterly failed; both succumbed to their illnesses and died in tragic ways.

A handmade Christmas card Elizabeth sent to her Aunt Grace in the 1970s

For Elizabeth, the repetition of childhood circumstances in adult life felt like a terrible cosmic joke. Moreover, she now experienced the one thing about her mother's life that had set her tragic childhood train in motion: the loss of her one great love too young, too soon. It did not help that Lota's family and many of their friends in Brazil blamed Elizabeth for the situation, for Lota's death, and turned against her.

Even though her sorrows were always close by, life in Brazil and with Lota had gone a long way towards Elizabeth's reconciliation with her past, because in Brazil she had been truly happy. But the final years, with Lota increasingly ill, with Elizabeth's own health deteriorating, much of the good progress eroded. Elizabeth was in a precarious state after Lota's death, desperate to keep her emotional train from derailing and putting her own life in jeopardy.

What began at this time was another period of dislocation and drifting, accompanied by an inability to write. Elizabeth lost not only her love, but also her home, a whole way of life, a place and time of happiness, stability, security, with its resultant creativity. Naturally, she wanted to stay connected to Brazil, even though she blamed the Brazilian government for working Lota into an early grave. Elizabeth felt a strong attachment to the parts of Brazil that had given her a home and the gifts of love and art.

She still had the Ouro Prêto house and her intention was to turn her attention to it, continue its restoration, and make it her Brazilian base. This desire remained strong for several years, but gradually she realized it was not only impractical, but also dangerous emotionally. Slowly, painfully, she extricated herself from the south. It took her a long time to leave for good, but eventually the north reclaimed her.

Elizabeth did not accompany Lota's body back to Rio. Dr. Baumann advised against it. She made plans to return in November to begin the difficult process of packing and moving her things and dealing with estate matters, made more unpleasant because Lota's sister contested the will. Just before leaving the United States, Elizabeth fell and broke her arm. Grief and drinking and disorientation took their toll.

This accident marked the beginning of a pattern of falls—she fell again and broke bones four or five times in the next decade. Alcohol was of course a factor. This falling phenomenon was, however, not entirely self-inflicted. It was also a condition that the women in her mother's family were prone to as they got older. Elizabeth herself told stories of Gammie's regular falls in her kitchen and on winter ice. Grace's daughter, Phyllis Sutherland, remembers her mother's numerous tumbles, especially down stairs. As Phyllis aged, she herself began to experience these unsettling accidents. Even Pa was known to fall.

The reason for these persistent mishaps (so frequent that they became part of family lore) is not known. Perhaps it was a balance problem, a genetic trait. Elizabeth was fifty-six when

Lota died, the right approximate age for the onset of this condition. Rarely, however, did the Bulmer women break bones. Grace was known to declare, "We fall but we don't break." For Elizabeth, her drinking was the added factor that took her falls to the breaking point.

Elizabeth's time in Brazil was unpleasant and brief. She returned to the United States on Christmas Eve 1967. Filled with grief, struggling with her health and injuries, terrified to be alone, she decided to move to San Francisco and live with Suzanne Bowen (a pseudonym), the young woman with whom she had had the affair in 1966. Suzanne was a single mother by this time, with a young son. She was capable, creative, and caring—all things Elizabeth needed in abundance. Suzanne helped Elizabeth manage her life and Elizabeth provided Suzanne and her son with a home. When they went to Ouro Prêto, Suzanne took charge of the house restoration.

Life in San Francisco in 1968 was nothing if not interesting, but the culture shock for Elizabeth was extreme, even with Suzanne as intermediary, and added to her disorientation. To distract herself, Elizabeth took Suzanne to Vancouver in May and they travelled across Canada by train. She hoped to make it to Nova Scotia but managed only Montreal, where she saw Aunt Mary, and where she got sick and was hospitalized for a week or so. She and Suzanne finally got as far as New York, where Elizabeth consulted with Dr. Baumann and reconnected with old friends. They returned to the West Coast by train through the United States.

Broken bones, illness, excessive drinking, and grief plagued Elizabeth in 1969. In February she suffered an ambiguous overdose of medication and alcohol, which frightened her and worried her friends. In the midst of all this trouble, however, she managed, with Suzanne's help, to put together and have published her *Complete Poems*. It won the National Book Award in 1970. Yet daily life in San Francisco, the renewed pressure to

> ## National Book Award
>
> The National Book Awards were initiated in 1950 and are presented each year to American authors for work published the previous year. Books are submitted for consideration by publishers in four categories: fiction, nonfiction, poetry, and young adult. Elizabeth won the award for poetry in March 1970. She was in Ouro Prêto, Brazil, at the time and was not able to return to the United States to accept the award, but she had a party to celebrate. Her friend and fellow poet Robert Lowell accepted the award on her behalf.

write, publish, and read publicly, and her own inner turmoil and drinking problem, combined to cause serious depression. She decided to retreat with Suzanne to Ouro Prêto.

Elizabeth and Suzanne's unlikely relationship was based on dependencies which over time put a great strain on their feelings for each other. In the isolation of Ouro Prêto, experiencing serious conflicts with the workmen who were restoring the house, with Suzanne's intensifying unhappiness and Elizabeth's unabated grief, their connection shattered. Their versions of cause and effect differed, but the outcome saw Suzanne return to the United States and Elizabeth remain in Brazil. Succumbing to one "black wave" of grief after another, Elizabeth was unsure what to do. She realized she had to sell her beloved Casa Mariana (named in honour of Marianne Moore) and leave Brazil for good. But where could she go?

Robert Lowell intervened again and arranged for her to take over his teaching post at Harvard University while he was living in Europe. It was a lifeline thrown out into her darkness, saving her from shipwreck, and she grabbed hold of it. As doubtful as she was about teaching writing, Elizabeth knew she had to get control of herself and her life. Just before flying back to the

The Great Village that Elizabeth Bishop returned to in the 1970s

United States in September 1970, writing to Dr. Baumann, she stated, perhaps as much to convince herself as the doctor, "I want to do it, too."

Elizabeth's first months in Cambridge were not encouraging. She had to return to San Francisco to close up her apartment. It was a short, lonely trip eased only by the help of her friend Dorothee Bowie. Severing from Suzanne was necessary, but Elizabeth still felt concerned about her and her son. When Suzanne appeared in Cambridge in October, Elizabeth was alarmed; but Suzanne only wanted references because she was going back to school to study medicine. Elizabeth provided her with a reference and some financial support and with that their contact ended.

Her first months at Harvard saw Elizabeth living in Kirkland House. Its administrative assistant was Alice Methfessel, another young, bright, capable woman. Almost immediately, Elizabeth began to rely on Alice as she had Suzanne. Their friendship

Honorary Degrees

With the awards and prizes mounting, it was not long after her return to the United States that Elizabeth began to receive honorary degrees. In the decade before her death she received degrees from Smith College (1969), Brown University (1972), Rutgers University (1972), Dalhousie University (1979), and Princeton University (1979). She said of the honorary degree given by Dalhousie University in May 1979 that it "rather pleased" her. Phyllis Sutherland and her family were present at the convocation.

quickly intensified and a settled relationship emerged. Alice was a calm, steady presence, but Elizabeth's dependence sometimes caused friction, and at least one major temporary separation. However, they remained together until Elizabeth's death. It was a loving bond which brought happiness and security to her final years.

One of the renewed pleasures of living in New England was the proximity to Nova Scotia. Elizabeth immediately began regular trips to the province which continued until her death. The first of these was in mid-October 1970, when she went to help celebrate Aunt Grace's eighty-first birthday.

Although Brazil was receding from her life (the suicide in 1971 of Lota's beloved nephew Flavio Soares, whom Elizabeth also adored, was one more tragic cut of the tie), she returned a few more times in the early 1970s, as she moved towards selling her house—a transaction that did not, in fact, happen until after her death. When she returned from a trip there in the spring of 1971, she was diagnosed with "amoebic dysentery plus three other kinds too (marvelous names, I must say). After all these years in the tropics!" In a way similar to the allergic reaction that initiated her life in Brazil in 1951–1952, which instituted an immunity to native ailments, the onslaught of these tropical diseases marked her departure from the south.

CITATION

Mr. President:

    I have the honour to present Elizabeth Bishop, a distinguished poet and friend of Nova Scotia.

    In recognition of the pleasure and enlightenment she has brought to many through her work, I ask you, Mr. President, on behalf of the Senate, to confer upon her the degree of Doctor of Laws, *honoris causa.*

Elizabeth Bishop

    Elizabeth Bishop was born in Worcester, Massachussetts, of Maritime parentage (her father was from Prince Edward Island, her mother from Great Village, Nova Scotia). Because of her father's sudden death and her mother's illness, Miss Bishop spent her early years at the home of her maternal grandparents in Great Village. She has travelled much and lived for many years in Brazil, but the mark of the Nova Scotia years is discernable in the setting, the imagery and the temper of some of her most memorable work.

    No American poet of our time has been more honoured than Elizabeth Bishop. She has won the Houghton Mifflen Award, the National Book Award, the National Book Critics Circle Award, and is the first woman and the first North American to win the Books Abroad/Neustadt Award for Literature. In 1976 she was elected to the American Academy of Arts and Letters whose membership is limited to fifty persons. She is also a member of the National Institute of Arts and Letters and a chancellor of the Academy of American Poets. Honorary Doctorates have been conferred on her by Smith College, Brown University and Rutgers.

    Elizabeth Bishop's poetry is notable for its clarity of perception, its sculptured finish, its quiet but searching wit, its compassion, and its capacity to reveal the extraordinary in what had seemed to be the ordinary stuff of daily life.

Citation of Elizabeth's honorary degree from Dalhousie University, presented at the university's spring convocation ceremony in May 1979

    Living in the United States, Elizabeth again was immersed in the world of the professional poet and poetry: teaching, reading, publishing, and receiving awards, including honorary degrees, fellowships, and prizes. She was never comfortable with these obligations and attentions, and viewed them with some irony. (She said of all the honorary degree hoods she received that she could make a quilt out of them and paper her wall with the parchments.) Still, with a more secure daily life, Elizabeth settled into the north and began to come into her own as an American poet.

    At Harvard she was meeting and influencing a new generation of poets: Frank Bidart, Lloyd Schwartz, Dana Gioia,

Jane Shore, Jonathan Galassi, Kathleen Spivack, and Seamus Heaney, to name only a few. To a large degree, these and other poets of their generation (including Mark Strand, Ashley Brown, Sandra MacPherson, Robert Pinsky, and Thom Gunn), served Elizabeth's memory and legacy well, keeping her name and influence current and relevant. As they themselves gained stature and influence, their advocacy helped spread her influence to even younger generations.

She also re-established regular contact with her many old friends, those writers and artists from her own generation. In particular, when Lowell returned from his sojourn in England and Ireland, they often met. Theirs was a vital friendship that had lasted over time and space and numerous personal tragedies.

Once her health stabilized, Elizabeth and Alice also travelled regularly—to Nova Scotia and Maine, of course, but also to places as far-flung as the Galápagos Islands, Norway, and Russia. One of the most exciting developments as she worked

Letter writing

Elizabeth taught at Harvard University for several years in the 1970s, primarily creative writing and poetry courses. She also developed a course about letter writing, which she was quite proud of and said was her favourite to teach. She introduced students to a wide range of letter writers, including Coleridge, Keats, and her own Aunt Grace. One of Elizabeth's favourite types of books to read was collections of letters, and she was an avid practitioner of the epistolary art her entire life. Thousands of her letters survive, and are now being published in their own collections.

to establish a place for herself in the north was the purchase in 1973–1974 of a condominium in Lewis Wharf, a restored nineteenth-century stone warehouse overlooking Boston Harbor. She told Dr. Baumann, "It's curious but true that ships from Nova Scotia used to dock here—perhaps even my great-grandfather's—and that all the granite was quarried in Quincy, the home of my ancestors on the *other* side of the family—near Boston."

Elizabeth was also writing again, and in December 1976 *Geography III*, what turned out to be her final collection, appeared. The poems in this small volume are some of the most important of her life: "In the Waiting Room," "Crusoe in England," "The Moose," "12 O'Clock News," "Poem," "One Art," "The End of March." They are also some of her most directly autobiographical poems, contemplations of her life as an artist. She also received the prestigious Books Abroad/Neustadt International Prize for Literature earlier that year. Her stature was solid and growing.

She struggled with poor health in 1977, a year which also brought her two more devastating losses. On August 22, at the age of eighty-eight, Aunt Grace died, the last real Bulmer (Aunt Mary had died in 1972). Barely three weeks later, on September 12, Robert Lowell died suddenly and unexpectedly. Her moving elegy for him, "North Haven" (after a place in Maine where they had spent time together), concluded, "The words won't change again. Sad friend, you cannot change." Elizabeth had already honoured her Aunt Grace by dedicating "The Moose" to her.

These deaths and worry about her own health made for a shaky 1978, even though Elizabeth kept on teaching and in March learned that she had been granted a $25,000 Guggenheim Fellowship. The first part of 1979 was more or less a steady round of readings, travel, socializing, and writing. In May she made what was her last visit to Nova Scotia, to receive

Elizabeth Bishop's gravestone at Hope Cemetery, Worcester, Massachusetts

an honorary degree from Dalhousie University. She wrote to Dorothee Bowie, "This one rather pleases me." Immediately afterwards, she and Alice took a cruise of the Greek Islands, a much-longed-for trip. She was ill again later that summer, but was clearly looking to a future of writing when in July she purchased the thirteen-volume *Oxford English Dictionary*. Sadly, she did not use it very long. On October 6, 1979, as she prepared to go out for supper with friends, Elizabeth Bishop died suddenly in her Lewis Wharf apartment of a cerebral aneurysm.

Elizabeth Bishop House in Great Village, as it is today, a quiet retreat for visiting artists

CHAPTER EIGHT

"OUR EARTHLY TRUST…"
A POET'S STATURE

For all her childhood tragedies and emotional and physical struggles, for all her self-doubt and questioning of her abilities, it is clear that Elizabeth Bishop had her individual poetic voice early in life. The poems and stories published in school magazines in the late 1920s are remarkably precocious and accomplished. From this time forward, she decided for herself which great literature to read and thought deeply about the writer's life.

As soon as her work began to be published, she also thought about how to present it. So frustrated were she and her classmates at Vassar with the stylistic restrictions of its literary publications, they created one of their own, *Con Spirito*, an act of significant independence. This interest in presentation (in fonts, paper, cover art, and design) was lifelong, speaking to a keen aesthetic self-consciousness. More than once Elizabeth said she would rather have been a painter.

Professional and public interest in Elizabeth and her art began in earnest with the first editors who, in the 1930s, chose her poems and stories for their journals. In her senior year at Vassar she read Marianne Moore's work. She was intrigued by Moore's utterly individual voice, as individual as that of Hopkins. Shy as she was, when Elizabeth learned that the college librarian knew Moore, she made a determined effort to meet this established writer. They connected instantly and a strong friendship followed. Moore recognized Elizabeth's talent and introduced her to the literary establishment, arranging for Elizabeth's work to appear in *Trial Balances* (1935), her first book publication. Moore's patronage was significant and beneficial, and for some years Elizabeth conscientiously deferred to her mentor. But the independent thinker, the young poet who had powerful life experience and a keen intellect, who had a distinct curiosity about the world and art (which sometimes paralleled Moore's and sometimes did not) eventually broke away:

> What I'm about to say, I'm afraid, will sound like ELIZABETH KNOWS BEST....But I can't seem to bring myself to give up the set form, which I'm afraid you think fills the poem with redundancies, etc. I feel that the rather rattletrap rhythm is appropriate....

Though framed in deferential language, these words by the twenty-nine-year-old Elizabeth were a declaration of independence as she defended her anti-war poem "Roosters." It is a testament to the depth of their friendship that Moore accepted it and continued to support Elizabeth's poetic effort.

Publication led to wider recognition, which led to meeting more writers, especially her contemporaries; but frequent travel and a preference for living outside urban centres removed her from the active literary scene—a realm in which she was always uncomfortable. Elizabeth was also a slow writer, a result of many factors (a high standard verging on perfectionism, self-doubt, restlessness, frequent illness). In spite or because of these factors, the work she completed was so good that it usually found a home.

Even though she suffered writer's block on a regular basis and was sometimes ill for long stretches, somehow she kept offering work to the world. Any writer who struggles with self-doubt knows what a remarkable feat it is to keep going. By the early 1940s, Elizabeth was a new and exciting voice in the American literary world. The next big development was the Houghton Mifflin prize, which brought the publication of her first book, *North & South*, in 1946. This book received significant attention, particularly from the young literary lion Robert Lowell.

Their friendship was one of the most important, personally and professionally, of her life. The support and service Lowell gave Elizabeth in print and in kind (securing funding and positions) was unstinting and invaluable, even when the commitments required of her made her uncomfortable. With *North & South*, Elizabeth was poised to enter a full-blown literary career in the United States. The year in Washington, D.C. (1949–1950) when she achieved the pinnacle of American poetry, a term as the Poetry Consultant for the Library of Congress (Poet Laureate), which could have been parlayed into all manner of opportunities, was so difficult that instead it triggered panic and depression.

The brochure for a conference on Elizabeth Bishop, held at Acadia University in Wolfville, Nova Scotia, September 1998

With success comes expectation from one's self and from others. Feeling that her literary output was lacking and that she could not produce in the expected way, at the expected rate, she decided to flee, first to Nova Scotia and then to anywhere else in the world. She landed in Brazil, and its exotic yet familiar culture (speaking to her of the rural Nova Scotia of her childhood) and the deep love and strong bond with Lota de Macedo Soares, who gave her the first real home of her adulthood, allowed her to settle down, to live and write and publish more comfortably than ever before.

The Elizabeth Bishop Society of Nova Scotia

The Elizabeth Bishop Society of Nova Scotia was formed in 1994 by a group of Bishop scholars, readers, and fans. It is based in Great Village, but has an international membership averaging 125–130 per year. It publishes an annual newsletter. Its website is: www.elizabethbishopns.org

Being distant from the literary clamour gave her a unique perspective and confidence to pursue an independent path. It also, at times, caused her self-doubt to kick in and intensified a sense of isolation. As early as 1933, Elizabeth identified her contradictory nature, which affected her writing process: "The trouble is, I can't get anything done when there are people here, but neither can I get anything done alone. After a few days, I sink into melancholia." Her first decade in Brazil gave her an ideal combination of both people and solitude, a workable balance that suited her needs.

Distance from the main currents of American culture had an impact on her presence in its formal institutions. She was separated from the usual paths that brought recognition and established reputation, but she continued to succeed and reached another pinnacle in 1956 when she won the Pulitzer Prize for Poetry. By the 1950s, with steady publication in magazines such as *The New Yorker* and regular awards and honours coming her way, Elizabeth was part of the American literary establishment, even if a minor figure, with a growing readership. Whereas in the 1930s she had written about her literary heroes and sought to connect with mentors and peers, now she was being written about and sought by peers and younger writers. While she never had the stature of Robert Lowell during their lifetime, her quiet, determined persistence, her high standards and independence, put her on solid literary ground. She planted her poems well and they have blossomed in each subsequent generation.

In January 1954, Elizabeth received what was surely one of her first fan letters, from Victor L. O. Chittick, who lived in Seattle and was professor emeritus of Reed College, Portland, Oregon. Chittick and his wife, Edna, were from Hantsport, Nova Scotia (across the bay from Great Village). He graduated from Acadia University not long before her great-uncle William Bernard Hutchinson was president there. Chittick read her stories "Gwendolyn" and "In the Village" in *The New Yorker* in 1953. He was so affected by them that his long initial letter gushed with praise and his own childhood memories:

> My competence in that field [aesthetic qualities] is much too amateur to put into words what I feel about the perfection of your writing. I am simply overwhelmed with its loveliness. But as a former Nova Scotian I should like to thank you for the delight you have given me with the absolutely correct Nova Scotianness of your characters, scenes, and incidents. Indeed you bring my past so much alive that you make me feel you have almost lived my youth over again.

Elizabeth's first letter to Chittick (she maintained a correspondence with him and Edna into the 1970s) does not survive, but his second to her, in March 1954, does. In it he asked her permission to write an essay about her work, and she agreed. The essay, published in the summer 1955 issue of the *Dalhousie Review*, was titled "Nomination for Laureateship." Based on what he had read in *The New Yorker*, on *North & South*, and on information and manuscript poems she provided, Chittick nominated Elizabeth Bishop "Nova Scotia's unofficial laureate." He could not have known, and no evidence exists to show that Elizabeth told him, that her Walnut Hill classmates had prophesied the position for her in 1929.

North & South received important reviews from the likes of Randall Jarrell and Robert Lowell, but Chittick's lengthy essay

The brochure for an international conference on Elizabeth Bishop's work, held in Ouro Prêto, Brazil, May 1999

was arguably the first major critical work about Elizabeth's art and proclaimed its Nova Scotianness. The next significant contribution to Bishop criticism was Anne Stevenson's book eleven years later.

By the early 1970s, like so many of her peers, Elizabeth realized the necessity of having a steady teaching job. She again entered the literary academy at another pinnacle: Harvard University. This shift brought her into active contact with a younger generation of poets. Wanting to be close to the centre of the poetry scene and studying with poet-celebrities such as Lowell, these young writers connected reluctantly with Elizabeth at first, but were usually won over by her genuineness. Her stature was such that by the late 1970s, her poetry had become, much to her bemusement, the subject of Ph.D. dissertations.

Elizabeth's premature death in 1979 came when she was at her artistic height. She was writing her most masterful poems. Her position in the American poetry scene was growing, even if she was still regarded as a minor poet, partly because of her relatively small amount of published work. Not long after her death, however, interest in Elizabeth Bishop's art and life underwent a dramatic expansion. Since the late 1980s hundreds of theses, dissertations, articles, and books have been written about her work, mostly, but not exclusively, in the United States, by poets, critics, and scholars. Several major biographical monographs

Poet Laureate

Appointed annually by the Librarian of Congress, the Poet Laureate position in the United States has been in existence since 1937, first with the title "Consultant in Poetry to the Library of Congress" and from 1986 onward as "Poet Laureate Consultant in Poetry." There have been nearly fifty Poets Laureate since the position was established. The United Kingdom has had a Poet Laureate position since the seventeenth century, and in Canada the Canadian Parliamentary Poet Laureate position was created in 2001. Today, there are many poet laureate positions across North America at the city and provincial/state level.

have appeared and her work has been the subject of several major conferences.

So marked was the increased interest in Elizabeth by the mid-1990s that Thomas Travisano, one of the first scholars to publish a book about her after her death, offered a specific examination of the reasons for this rise to prominence, for the emergence of what he called "The Elizabeth Bishop Phenomenon." Travisano identified five factors—a shift in the attitudes of readers, a shift in academic interests, an increase of biographical information, an increase of appreciation for the quality of the work, and the influence of important advocates—that combined to cause this phenomenon. Travisano argues that Elizabeth Bishop's increasing popularity is not meteoric (a flash in the night sky), but rather a "Big Bang" (the creation of a new universe).

By this point in the story, the turn of the twenty-first century, Elizabeth Bishop had acquired canonical status; that is, acceptance as a major literary force in the academy, especially in the United States, the country that stakes the biggest claim to her (she was born, died, and is buried there). However, Canada and Brazil can also lay strong claims to Elizabeth Bishop, who was one of the few truly Pan-American poets of the twentieth century. These claims have been slower to materialize.

Elizabeth Bishop House

In 2004 a group of Elizabeth Bishop fans bought her childhood home in Great Village, Nova Scotia, and since then they have shared this special place with many artists. There is a "house journal" in which artists in residence write. One of these artists is poet and novelist Anne Simpson. On Thursday, November 22, 2007, she wrote:

> How much I liked coming into the kitchen! This house is such a wonderful, familiar farmhouse, but it's the kitchen I love (this has been the place where I've worked). It reminds me of my grandmother's kitchen. I almost expected to find a wringer washer it the laundry/bathroom. I've been here to write an essay for a book on place and poetics. I'm intending to write about the Elizabeth Bishop House….

Anne did write that essay, "World at Play," which was published in the collection *The Marram Grass: Poetry & Otherness* in 2009.

Victor Chittick's insightful 1955 essay was not followed up. Individual Canadian writers and readers knew her or knew of her work, but Chittick was so frustrated by the silence about her in Canada that in the late 1960s he drafted another essay, "Nomination Seconded," which he sent to Elizabeth. Sadly, he died soon after and it was never published. The silence continued in Canada until the 1980s (though it must be pointed out that it was Quebec writer Marie Claire Blais who sponsored Elizabeth for the Neustadt Prize in the mid-1970s). Poet and scholar David Staines, who knew Elizabeth at Harvard in the 1970s and who introduced her to the famous Canadian literary critic Northrop Frye, marked her death with a memorial essay in *Canadian Poetry* in 1980. With the publication of *The Complete Poems, 1929–1979* (1983) and *The Collected Prose* (1984), Maritime writers and literary scholars began to pay attention. Essays by poet Peter Sanger and cultural geographer Brian Robinson in the mid-1980s were the first real signs of change in Canada. I published my first essay about Elizabeth's childhood in Nova Scotia in 1991, and other scholars and poets soon followed.

The 1990s also saw the formation of two societies: the Elizabeth Bishop Society in the United States and the Elizabeth Bishop Society of Nova Scotia. Comprised of academics, scholars, artists, and readers from around the world, these organizations' efforts have reflected and contributed to the growing awareness of her significance.

In the 1980s Vassar College began an active program of purchasing her papers, especially letters and manuscripts. A major portion of their Elizabeth Bishop Papers came directly from her estate, but collecting occurred across North America, including in Nova Scotia. Letters and manuscripts are regarded as the most important literary remains of a writer, but these documents are not the only valuable records. In the 1990s I spent several years identifying and describing the archival record connected to Elizabeth and her maternal family found in Nova Scotia. A significant portion of this material was deposited at Acadia University Archives and has since been digitized.

A program for a session on Elizabeth Bishop, part of *The New Yorker* Festival in 2002

Another marker of an artist's stature (both popular and academic) is pilgrimage: devoted readers and scholars travelling to sites important to the artist, including their birth place, grave site, and homes. Sites significant to Elizabeth are found all along her north-south axis: Great Village, Worcester, Key West, Ouro Prêto. In the early 1980s, the residents of Great Village began to notice such pilgrims. There has been an increasing number of them ever since, devoted readers keen to visit Elizabeth's childhood home and walk the roads of her Nova Scotian village. So important is her childhood home in Great Village that the Nova Scotia government designated it a Provincial Heritage Property in 1997.

Perhaps the greatest marker of the excellence and influence of an artist is when other artists respond to her life and work, incorporate or pay tribute to her in their own art. Composers have set Elizabeth's texts to music, some of which she herself heard. Painters painted her likeness during her lifetime and since her death. Well-known photographers took her photograph, and since her death others have captured her beloved landscapes and homes. Playwrights from Nova Scotia, New York, and Rio de Janeiro have dramatized her life. Novels are now being written about it. Filmmakers have documented it. Translators have published her poems and stories in over a dozen languages. Most important of all, countless poets around the world have been inspired by her, dedicating poems to her, weaving her lines and images into new poems, and reading her work aloud in public for the sheer joy of it.

With Elizabeth Bishop's hundredth birthday—her centenary—in 2011, her stature as one of the most important poets of the twentieth century is secure. What is it about Elizabeth Bishop that draws so many people to her art? The answer to that question is different for each reader. For me, the answer is both simple and complex. I regard Elizabeth Bishop as a brilliantly gifted writer and a deeply humane person. The excellence of her craft is equalled by her compassion and wisdom. She looks death and loss directly in the face; she feels and writes their weight. Yet she also holds onto a belief in the essential goodness of life and finds humour and irony in the very failings she confronts and describes. Life is impermanent, uncertain, filled with unanswerable questions, but Elizabeth Bishop kept asking the questions and quietly offering her insights into the mystery and surprise.

The epigraph on her gravestone in Worcester, Massachusetts, her favourite line from all her poetry, which appears in "The Bight," reads:

> All the untidy activity continues,
> awful but cheerful.

The plaque commemorating Elizabeth Bishop's life and work, and her connection to Nova Scotia, erected in Great Village in 1992

EPILOGUE

"HOME-MADE, HOME-MADE! BUT AREN'T WE ALL?"

WHEN WE have the trajectory of an entire life before us, we can survey it, identify turning points, locate inevitable or accidental events, take stock of and interpret choices and outside influences. Biographers reconstruct the whole from the many parts and recreate the life story that was known only imperfectly in the actual living of it. This kind of effort can only be approximate—we can see someone else only through the lens of our own experience, analyze and judge only from a subjective point of view. As Elizabeth Bishop observed near the end of her life, it takes an "infinite number of things" coming together to create art. Even full-scale, multi-volume biographies can account for only a fraction of these things. This brief biography of Elizabeth Bishop recounts her life by focusing on certain events, people, and aspects, in particular her connections to Nova Scotia and her maternal family. This book can tell only part of her story.

Elizabeth Bishop knew that just as she was interested in the

Elizabeth Bishop in front of the Presbyterian church in Great Village, Nova Scotia, *circa* 1916

Elizabeth Bishop at Balmoral Grist Mill, Balmoral, Nova Scotia, 1970s

writers whose work she read, others would be interested in her. She may not have been comfortable with this fact (she preferred privacy), but she understood it. She had a clear sense that others would not only read her work but want to read about her life, and that it helped to know something about her life to understand her work.

Common sense tells us that life and art are connected. Without life—our human life—there is no art. Art is a uniquely human phenomenon. Life and art inform—and even imitate—each other in many ways.

Elizabeth spoke directly about this idea in a late poem titled "Poem," about a little painting of Great Village done by her Great-Uncle George. She owned the painting. It hung in her kitchen at Lewis Wharf. She identified with the painter and connected herself to the scene he had painted decades before she was born:

> Our visions coincided — "visions" is
> too serious a word — our looks, two looks:
> art "copying from life" and life itself,
> life and the memory of it so compressed
> they've turned into each other. Which is which?
> Life and the memory of it cramped,
> dim, on a piece of Bristol board,
> dim, but how live, how touching in detail
> — the little that we get for free,
> the little of our earthly trust. Not much.
> About the size of our abidance….

    Another late poem, "Crusoe in England," concerns, among many things, the place and purpose of the artist in the world. Crusoe is shipwrecked on a lonely island and must improvise his daily and imaginative life based on what natural and inner resources are available. As Crusoe builds a world for himself, he realizes that it happens because of his own creativity, and asks, "Home-made, home-made! But aren't we all?" It is critical that this observation is a question. Elizabeth Bishop allows Crusoe, and all of us, not only to hold the mystery, the uncertainty, and the infinite possibilities of what we are made of, but also to keep them open-ended. She *asks* us what we are made of, she does not *tell* us, and her poetic biography of Crusoe offers insights into her and our own answers to this question. In the deepest, widest, and most mysterious sense of this idea, Elizabeth Bishop was a truly remarkable home-made poet.

SELECTED BIBLIOGRAPHY

BY ELIZABETH BISHOP

North & South. Boston: Houghton Mifflin, 1946.
Poems: North & South / A Cold Spring. Boston: Houghton Mifflin, 1955.
Questions of Travel. New York: Farrar, Straus and Giroux, 1965.
The Complete Poems. New York: Farrar, Straus and Giroux, 1969.
Geography III. New York: Farrar, Straus and Giroux, 1976.
The Complete Poems, 1927–1979. New York: Farrar, Straus and Giroux, 1983.
The Collected Prose. New York: Farrar, Straus and Giroux, 1984.
One Art: Letters. Edited by Robert Giroux. New York: Farrar, Straus and Giroux, 1994.
Conversations with Elizabeth Bishop. Edited by George Montiero. Jackson: University Press of Mississippi, 1996.
Exchanging Hats: Elizabeth Bishop Paintings. Edited by William Benton. New York: Farrar, Straus and Giroux, 1996.
Edgar Allan Poe & the Juke-Box: Uncollected Poems, Drafts, and Fragments. Edited by Alice Quinn. New York: Farrar, Straus and Giroux, 2006.
Bishop: Poems, Prose, and Letters. New York: The Library of America, 2008.
Words in Air: The Complete Correspondence Between Elizabeth Bishop and Robert Lowell. Edited by Thomas Travisano with Saskia Hamilton. New York: Farrar, Straus and Giroux, 2008.
Elizabeth Bishop and The New Yorker: The Complete Correspondence. Edited by Joelle Biele. New York: Farrar, Straus and Giroux, 2011.

ABOUT AND INSPIRED BY ELIZABETH BISHOP

Anderson, Linda, and Jo Shapcott. *Elizabeth Bishop: Poet of the Periphery*. Tarset, Northumberland, U.K.: Bloodaxe Books, 2002.
Barry, Sandra, Gwendolyn Davies, Peter Sanger, eds. *Divisions of the Heart: Elizabeth Bishop and the Art of Memory and Place*. Kentville, N.S.: Gaspereau Press, 2001.

Costello, Bonnie. *Elizabeth Bishop: Questions of Mastery*. Cambridge, MA: Harvard University Press, 1991.

Fountain, Gary, and Peter Brazeau, eds. *Elizabeth Bishop: An Oral Biography*. Amherst: University of Massachusetts Press, 1994.

Goldensohn, Lorrie. *Elizabeth Bishop: The Biography of a Poetry*. New York: Columbia University Press, 1992.

Harrison, Victoria. *Elizabeth Bishop's Poetics of Intimacy*. Cambridge: Cambridge University Press, 1993.

Kalstone, David. *Becoming a Poet: Elizabeth Bishop with Marianne Moore and Robert Lowell*. New York: Farrar, Straus and Giroux, 1989.

Millier, Brett. *Elizabeth Bishop: Life and the Memory of It*. Berkeley: University of California Press, 1993.

Oliveira, Carmen. *Rare and Commonplace Flowers: The Story of Elizabeth Bishop and Lota De Macedo Soares*. Translated by Neil Besner. New Brunswick, NJ: Rutgers University Press, 2002.

Pickard, Zachariah. *Elizabeth Bishop's Poetics of Description*. Montreal and Kingston: McGill-Queen's University Press, 2008.

Schwartz, Lloyd and Sybil P. Estess, eds., *Elizabeth Bishop and Her Art*. Ann Arbor: The University of Michigan Press, 1983.

Sledge, Michael. *The More I Owe You*. Berkeley: Counterpoint, 2010. (a novel)

Smyth, Donna. *Running to Paradise*. Kentville, N.S.: Gaspereau Press, 1999. (a play)

Stevenson, Anne. *Five Looks at Elizabeth Bishop*. London: Bellew, 1998.

Travisano, Thomas. *Elizabeth Bishop: Her Artistic Development*. Charlottesville: University Press of Virginia, 1988.

SOURCES
CHAPTER TITLES

Prologue – "an infinite number of things"
Letter to Jerome Mazzaro, April 27, 1978. *One Art: Elizabeth Bishop Letters*. Edited by Robert Giroux. New York: Farrar, Straus, and Giroux, 1994, p. 621.

Chapter One – "That line of my family"
Letter from Elizabeth Bishop to Anne Stevenson, March 18, 1963. Elizabeth Bishop Collection. Olin Library, Washington University, St. Louis, Missouri.

Chapter Two – "the elements speaking"
Elizabeth Bishop. "In the Village." *The Collected Prose*. New York: Farrar, Straus, and Giroux, 1984, p. 274.

Chapter Three – "That Nova Scotian village"
Elizabeth Bishop. "In the Village." *The Collected Prose*. New York: Farrar, Straus, and Giroux, 1984, p. 251.

Chapter Four – "You are an *I*"
Elizabeth Bishop. "In the Waiting Room." *The Complete Poems*, 1927–1979. New York: Farrar, Straus, and Giroux, 1983, p. 160.

Chapter Five – "Long leagues of thee"
Elizabeth Bishop. "Three Sonnets for the Eyes." *The Complete Poems*, 1927–1979. New York: Farrar, Straus, and Giroux, 1983, p. 224.

Chapter Six – " Driving to the interior"
Elizabeth Bishop. "Arrival at Santos." *The Complete Poems*, 1927–1979. New York: Farrar, Straus, and Giroux, 1983, p. 90.

Chapter Seven – "Nature repeats herself"
Elizabeth Bishop. "North Haven." *The Complete Poems*, 1927–1979. New York: Farrar, Straus, and Giroux, 1983, p.188.

Chapter Eight – "Our earthly trust"
Elizabeth Bishop. "Poem." *The Complete Poems*, 1927–1979. New York: Farrar, Straus, and Giroux, 1983, p. 177.

Epilogue – "Home-made, home-made! But aren't we all?"
Elizabeth Bishop. "Crusoe in England." *The Complete Poems*, 1927–1979. New York: Farrar, Straus, and Giroux, 1983, p. 164.

TEXT

Reprinted by permission of Farrar, Straus and Giroux, LLC:

Excerpts from THE COLLECTED PROSE by Elizabeth Bishop. Copyright © 1984 by Alice Helen Methfessel. Excerpts from THE COMPLETE POEMS 1927-1979 by Elizabeth Bishop. Copyright © 1979, 1983 by Alice Helen Methfessel. Excerpts from PROSE by Elizabeth Bishop. Copyright © 2011 by The Alice H. Methfessel Trust. Editor's Note and compilation copyright © 2011 by Lloyd Schwartz.

Excerpts from ONE ART: LETTERS by Elizabeth Bishop, selected and edited by Robert Giroux. Copyright © 1994 by Alice Methfessel. Introduction and compilation copyright © 1994 by Robert Giroux.

Reprinted by permission of Farrar, Straus and Giroux, LLC on behalf of the Elizabeth Bishop Estate:

Excerpts from unpublished letters and unfinished novel "Reminiscences of Great Village" by Elizabeth Bishop. Copyright © 2009 Alice Helen Methfessel.

IMAGES

All images courtesy of the Bulmer-Bowers-Hutchinson-Sutherland fonds, Esther Clark Wright Archives, Acadia University, with the following exceptions:

Collection of Sandra Barry: 2, 37, 44 (bottom), 48, 49, 63, 78–79, 81, 82, 97, 101, 104, 107

Courtesy of Ann Marie Duggan: 84, 85

Courtesy of Laurie Gunn: 98, 110

Courtesy of James Jaffe: v (centre), 16

Collection of Meredith and Robert Layton: 32, 35, 36, 39, 44 (top), 86, 92

Collection of Helen MacLachlan: 38

Courtesy of Nova Scotia Archives and Records Management: 25

Courtesy of Special Collections, Vassar College Libraries: 12, 47, 72

Reproduced with the permission of Vassar College: iii, 60, 66

Courtesy of Yarmouth County Museum and Archives: 53

http://home.cc.umanitoba.ca/~wyatt/alltime/pics/acadiantt1946.html: 74

INDEX

A

Acadia University 15, 101, 103
Acadia University Archives 107
Amazon River 83
Andrade, Carlos Drummond de 83
Anthology of Twentieth-Century Brazilian Poetry 83
"Armadillo, The" 76
"Arrival at Santos" 76
"At the Fishhouses" 34, 74
Avalon Peninsula, NL 66

B

Balmoral, NS 112
"Baptism, The" 34
Barker, Ilse 1, 77
Barker, Kit 1, 77
Baudelaire, Charles 7
Baumann, Dr. Anny 2, 89, 90, 92, 96
Bay of Fundy 33, 34
Benton, William 82
Beppo (dog) 48
Bernlef, J. 16
Betsy (dog) 29, 37
Bidart, Frank 94
"Bight, The" 109
Bishop family 9, 12, 21, 30, 48, 50, 57, 61
Bishop, Florence Foster 10, 47, 48
Bishop, Gertrude Bulmer 17, 21–32, 48, 56, 61, 65, 74, 75, 87
Bishop, John, Jr. (Jack) 47, 48, 57, 64
Bishop, John Wilson 10, 12, 13, 17, 26, 30, 47, 50, 57, 64
Bishop, Ruby 48
Bishop, Sarah Foster 10, 12, 17, 30, 47, 57
Bishop, William 12
Bishop, William Thomas 17, 21–24
Black, Mary Elizabeth 13
Blais, Marie Claire 106
Blough, Frani 58, 64, 65
Blue Pencil 2, 58
Books Abroad/Neustadt International Prize for Literature 96, 106
Boomer (as var. of Bulmer) 12
Boston Harbor 96

Boston, MA 21, 24, 51, 53, 74, 96
Bowen, Suzanne 90–92
Bowers, Grace Bulmer 4, 11, 12, 19, 22, 44, 51–53, 55, 61–62, 73, 75, 78, 88–90, 93, 95, 96
Bowers, William 61
Bowie, Dorothee 92, 97
Bowplate, SS 2, 79, 80
Brant, Senhora Augusto Mario Caldeira 83
Brasil, Emanuel 83
Brazil 1, 2, 5, 43, 69, 75, 76, 79–93, 101, 102, 105
"Brazil, January 1, 1502" 76
Brown, Ashley 95
Browning, Robert 36, 55
Brown University 93
Bulmer, Arthur Bridges 32, 43, 56, 64
Bulmer, Elizabeth 17, 22, 28, 29, 45, 61
Bulmer family 8, 9, 11, 12, 18, 29, 33, 38, 42, 61
Bulmer, Horatio Nelson 11
Bulmer, John 11
Bulmer, Mabel 56
Bulmer, Mary Ann Maxfield 11
Bulmer, William Brown 11, 14, 17, 22, 28, 29, 32, 43, 61
"Burglar of Babylon, The" 76
Burns, Robert 36, 55

C

Cambridge, MA 92
Camp Chequessett 56, 57
Canadian Poetry 106
"Cape Breton" 34, 74
Cape Breton Island, NS 74
Cape Cod, MA 57, 62
Cardozo, Joaquim 83
Casa Mariana 84, 85, 91
Chesney, Barbara 58
Child's Garden of Verses, A 55
Chittick, Edna 103
Chittick, Victor L. O. 103, 106
Christophian Literary Society 36, 38, 55
Clark, Eleanor 7
Cobequid Bay 33
Cobequid Mountains 11, 33

Cold Spring, A 75
Coleridge, Samuel Taylor 95
Collected Prose 106
Collingwood, Joan 58
Complete Poems, The (1969) 90
Complete Poems, 1929-1979, The 106
Con Spirito 63, 99
"Country Mouse, The" 31, 47, 49
Crane, Louise 65, 67, 68, 69, 70, 81
"Crusoe in England" 5, 96, 113
Cumberland County 11

D

Dalhousie Review 103
Dalhousie University 93, 94, 97
Dante 36
Dartmouth, NS 25, 27
DesBrisay, Bligh 73
DesBrisay, Ella 73
Dewey, Jane 77
Dewey, John 77
Diamantina, Brazil 82, 83
Diary of 'Helena Morley', The 83
Dix, Dorothea 25
Doyle, Arthur Conan 14

E

Eliot, T. S. 63
Elizabeth Bishop 85
Elizabeth Bishop House 98, 106
Elizabeth Bishop Society 107
Elizabeth Bishop Society of Nova Scotia 102, 107
Elmcroft Farm 61, 73
Elmonte House, Great Village 30, 38
Elwood, Frank 56
"End of March, The" 96
Europe 5, 67
Exchanging Hats 82

F

Fales, Sarah Jane 10
Farwell, Harriet 57
"Filling Station" 34
"First Death in Nova Scotia" 34, 56
Florida 76, 77
Folly Village, NS 13
"For C.W.B." 34
Fortune's Wheel 13, 15, 83
Foster family 9–10
Foster, Reginald (or Reynold) 10
Foster, Sarah A. 10
Foster, Thomas R. 10
Francis, Billy 41
Francis, Reverend F. G. 37

Fraser, Reverend Alexander Louis 36
Frye, Northrop 106

G

Galápagos Islands 95
Galassi, Jonathan 95
Geography III 96
Gillespie, William 37
Gioia, Dana 94
Great Salem Fire 24
Great Village Baptist Church 36, 37
Great Village, NS 1, 5, 8, 13–14, 21, 24, 27, 30–45, 47, 50, 54–58, 61–62, 68, 73, 86, 92, 102–103, 106, 108, 112
Great Village River 33
Great Village School 37, 39, 40, 44
Greek Islands 97
Green Island 53
Green Mansions 2
Guggenheim Fellowship 96
Gunn, Thom 95
"Gwendolyn" 1, 34, 56, 103

H

Hale, Sheila 14
Halifax Explosion 29, 54
Halifax, NS 54, 73
Hantsport, NS 103
Harvard University 91–95, 104, 106
Heaney, Seamus 95
Herbert, George 7
History of Great Village, The 19
Hooper, Sarah 12
Hope Cemetery, Worcester, MA 97
Hopkins, Gerard Manley 7, 62, 99
Houghton Mifflin Poetry Award 70, 100
Hudson, W. H. 2
Huntington, Evelyn 66, 67
Hutchinson, Charles 13
Hutchinson, Elizabeth 13, 14
Hutchinson family 9, 13–15
Hutchinson, George Wylie 13, 14, 15, 16, 50, 67, 82, 112
Hutchinson, John Robert 13, 15, 83
Hutchinson, Mary 14
Hutchinson, Robert 8, 13, 14, 78, 80
Hutchinson, William Bernard 14, 15, 19, 103

I

Imo 29
"Insomnia" 74
"In the Village" 1, 28, 34, 81, 103
"In the Waiting Room" 48, 49, 96

J

Jarrell, Randall 75, 103
Johnson, Dr. T. R. 54

K

Kazin, Pearl 80
Keats, John 36, 95
Key West, FL 68–71, 81, 108
Kipling, Rudyard 14
Kirkland House, Harvard University 92

L

Lacerda, Carlos 83
"Large Bad Picture" 14, 34
Lewis Wharf, Boston 16, 96, 97, 113
Linkletter, Zilpha 73
Lispector, Clarice 83
Lockeport, NS 73
Lowell, Robert 7, 65, 75–77, 91, 95–96, 100–104

M

MacLachlan, Muir 40
MacPherson, Sandra 95
Maine 76, 95, 96
"Manners" 34
Mann, Margaret 58
"Manuelzinho" 76
Marblehead, MA 24
Marram Grass, the 106
Maryland 77
Maxfield, Mary Ann 11
Mazzaro, Jerome 3
McCarthy, Mary 7
Meade, Sarah 11
"Memories of Uncle Neddy" 34
Merrill, James 5
Methfessel, Alice 92–95, 97
Mexico 5, 69
Miller, Margaret 65, 67
Millier, Brett 71
Milton, John 36
Minas Basin 33
Minas Gerais, Brazil 81
Mina Vida de Menina 82
Mindlin, Henrique 83
"Miracle for Breakfast, A" 67
Modern Architecture in Brazil 83
Mont Blanc 29
Montreal, QC 61, 90
Moore, Marianne 7, 66, 70, 71, 85, 91, 99, 100
"Moose, The" 34, 74, 78, 96
Morash, Georgie 40, 41

Morley, Helena 82
Morse, Mary 80
Mount Hope, see Nova Scotia Hospital
"Mrs. Sullivan Downstairs" 53

N

Natick, MA 7, 57
National Book Award 90, 91
National Geographic Magazine 49
Newfoundland 66
New York City, NY 2, 21, 64, 67, 68, 69, 73, 76, 79, 80, 84, 85, 90, 108
New Yorker 1, 78, 82, 102, 103
New Yorker Festival 107
"North Haven" 96
North Shore Country Day School 57
North & South 70, 75, 100, 101, 103
North Star 53
Norway 95
Nova Scotia Hospital (Mount Hope) 25, 27, 29, 73
Nova Scotian Hotel 73

O

"One Art" 96
193rd Highland Brigade 41
Ouro Prêto, Brazil 78, 81, 84, 85, 89, 90, 91, 104, 108
"Over 2,000 Illustrations and a Complete Concordance" 34, 54
Owl 57
Oxford English Dictionary 97

P

Panama 21
Pansy (horse) 77
Paris, France 7
"Paris, 7 A.M." 67
Parque do Flamengo 83, 87
Patriquin, Gwendolyn 1, 56
Petrópolis, Brazil 80
"Pink Dog" 76
Pinsky, Robert 95
"Poem" 16, 34, 96, 112
Poems: North & South / A Cold Spring 54, 75, 82
Poet Laureate 76, 101, 105
Port of Londonderry 34
Poughkeepsie, NY 64
"Primer Class" 34, 40, 44
Princeton University 93
"Prodigal, The" 34, 75
Pulitzer, Joseph 75
Pulitzer Prize 54, 75, 82, 102

Q

"Quai d'Orleans" 67
"Questions of Travel" 76
Questions of Travel 82
Quincy, MA 96

R

"Reprimand, The" 34, 65
Revere, MA 5, 50, 51, 57
Rio de Janeiro, Brazil 7, 14, 80, 83, 84, 89, 108
"Riverman, The" 76
Robinson, Brian 106
"Roosters" 66, 100
Ross, Mary Bulmer 22, 40, 41, 61, 90, 96
Rukeyser, Muriel 7
Russia 95
Rutgers University 93

S

Sable Island, NS 14, 77, 78
Salem Harbor 24
Samambaia, Brazil 3, 72, 80, 81, 83
Sammy (toucan) 1, 72
"Sandpiper" 34
San Francisco, CA 90, 92
Sanger, Peter 106
"Santarém" 76
Santos, Brazil 80
Saratoga Springs, NY 77
Saugus High School 57
Saugus, MA 57
Schwartz, Lloyd 94
"Sea & Its Shore, The" 12
Seattle, WA 85, 103
Seaver, Robert 65
"Sestina" 34
Shakespeare, William 36
Shelley, Percy Bysshe 62
Shepherdson, George 21, 22, 50, 51, 54, 57, 61, 68, 69, 71
Shepherdson, Maude Bulmer 21, 22, 32, 50, 51–57, 61, 68, 69, 71, 82
Shore, Jane 95
Simpson, Anne 106
"Sleeping on the Ceiling" 67
Smith, Beryl 44
Smith College 93
Soares, Flavio 93
Soares, Lota de Macedo 1, 2, 3, 69, 72, 80–90, 93, 101
Spivack, Kathleen 95
Sponagle, J. E. 20
"Squatter's Children" 76

Staines, David 106
Stevens, Marjorie 65, 68, 74, 75, 76
Stevenson, Anne 4, 15, 23, 26, 44, 45, 84, 85, 104
Stevenson, Robert Louis 14, 55
St. James Presbyterian Church, Great Village 35–37
Strand, Mark 95
St. Vincent's Hospital, New York City 85
Sullivan, Rosemary 8
"Summer's Dream, A" 34
Sutherland, Phyllis 89
Swampscott, MA 57
Swenson, May 77

T

Tennyson, Alfred 36, 55
"Three Sonnets for the Eyes" 34
Time-Life 84
"Time's Andromedas" 16
"To a Tree" 61
"To the Botequim and Back" 76
Travisano, Thomas 105
Trial Balances 66, 70, 99
"Trip to Vigia, A" 76
"12 O'Clock News" 96

V

Vancouver, BC 90
Vassar College 5, 7, 16, 17, 18, 57, 59, 63–66, 99, 107
Vassarian 60, 64, 66
Vassar, Matthew 64

W

Walnut Hill School 2, 5, 7, 57–59, 62, 103
Wanning, Tom 76
Washington, D.C. 7, 77, 101
Washington, University of 85
Winslow, Ann 70
Worcester, MA 21, 30, 47, 48, 51, 108, 109
World War I 35, 41, 42, 45
World War II 45, 70

Y

Yaddo artist colony 77
Yarmouth, NS 53

Z

Zangwill, Israel 14

INDEX 121

STORIES OF OUR PAST SERIES

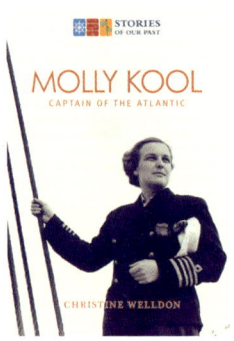